COCINA LIBRE

IMMIGRANT RESISTANCE RECIPES

Stories and food by immigrants and refugees

Dr. Julia Roncoroni
Dr. Delio Figueroa

Edited by Alana Goldberg

Center for Community Engagement
to Advance Scholarship and Learning

Table of

CONTENTS

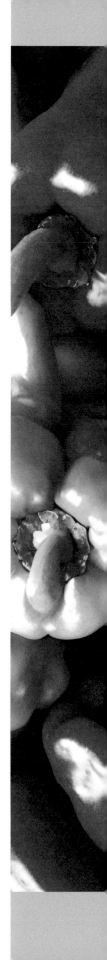

VEGETABLE STEW   65

Gloria Duran - Mexico

BLACK BEAN PUPUSAS   68

Claudia & Silvia Quijada - Metapan, El Salvador

LOROCO PUPUSAS   69

Claudia & Silvia Quijada - Metapan, El Salvador

SPINACH PUPUSAS   70

Claudia & Silvia Quijada - Metapan, El Salvador

ZUCCHINI PUPUSAS   71

Claudia & Silvia Quijada - Metapan, El Salvador

BANGLADESHI BEEF STEW   74

Shoeb Iqbal - Noakhali, Bangladesh

SPAGHETTI   78

Renato Fierro - Chihuahua, Mexico

MISER WAT   80

Senait Ketema - Dire Dawa, Ethiopia

YEKIK ALICHA   81

Senait Ketema - Dire Dawa, Ethiopia

TIKIL GOMEN   82

Senait Ketema - Dire Dawa, Ethiopia

EMPANADAS-POTATO/CHEESE 85

Guadalupe Lopez - La Blanca, Guatemala

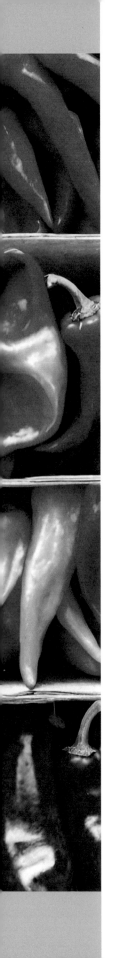

Foreword

CHEF BYRON GOMEZ

I am an immigrant. It is not only the stories and recipes documented on these pages, it is also the liaison that connected me to this book. My story is no different than the courageous and brave people in this book. As an immigrant, DACA recipient, and also a professional Chef this hits home. To me, the biggest act of love is cooking. It is a way of expressing and communicating when language and culture were barriers while residing in this country. The constant pressure of change, uncertainty, and feeling like I needed to keep up was a new adapted way of life. On the other hand, the fear of losing my identity, culture, and roots led me to uncertain grounds which questioned my authenticity of where I come from or where I am going.

Foreword

CONT'D

In the mists of all this turmoil, cooking and food kept me grounded. Sharing recipes with others gave me the confidence and smile I much needed at times just to get by each day. This struggle is what the immigrant community faces each day. That is why this book is so special. Flipping through the pages I had recollections of many first experiences I had through food. Gazing at pictures of hands hovering over Ethiopian Injera reminded me of being invited to my friend's home and tasting this traditional dish for the first time. The list goes on and on with the recipes in this book. This not only ignited a past acquaintance with a memory, but blossomed a smile on my face thinking about that place, time and feeling. Food breaks down any barrier, crumbles any walls or obstacles and catapults our courage to honor where we come from and who we are. It brings people together for educational purposes, nuances and just to connect as humans. Food speaks. The stories of each and every person involved with this book also tells its own beautiful story. A story we all need to hear but even better, a story we can taste.

If you are reading these words, my desire is that you have the impulse and inspiration to try some of these recipes. Like the immigrants and storytellers here, they found the courage to try something different. A new environment, culture, language and taste of and for life. You too can have that joy of life a recipe at a time, you can also share a new experience with your friends and family and you too can find great pleasure in cooking and telling your story.

This is the power of food.

Byron Gomez

ABOUT CIRC

All proceeds from this book will be donated to Colorado Immigrant Rights Coalition (CIRC). Here is their website: www.coloradoimmigrant.org

ABOUT CIRC

CIRC is a statewide, membership-based organization that advocates for all immigrants in Colorado and the United States, regardless of legal status. CIRC seeks to build community power through organizing and leadership development within immigrant communities, winning fair and humane public policies, providing legal services and educational workshops, and implementing non-partisan civic engagement programs.

CIRC PROGRAMS

- Advocacy for access to healthcare
- Advocacy for access to safe and affordable housing
- Federal advocacy for comprehensive immigration reform
- Community organizing & leadership development
- Voter education and civic engagement
- Direct legal services
- Deportation resistance

CIRC IMPACT

Led a statewide campaign to expand healthcare access for undocumented children and pregnant people.

Protected private personal data entrusted to state government agencies from access by third-party agencies, including ICE.

Launched their Legal Services to assist DACA recipients renew their status and LPRs become new citizens.

Passed a statewide legal defense fund, ensuring legal representation in deportation proceedings.

Launched the first statewide ICE abuse documentation hotline to collect data and testimonies.

Won driver's licenses for all (SB- 251) and continue to protect and expand this law.

A NOTE FROM CIRC

Thank you for your support!

We are deeply grateful to Julia & Delio for creating this beautiful cookbook and to all of the immigrants who contributed to it. This isn't just a collection of recipes and stories, but of traditions and dreams. We hope you find new recipes to cook, but also some parts of yourself—scents, flavors, colors, textures, sounds—that resonate and remind you of home, no matter how far it may be. We can all agree that cooking is an act of love, and sharing a meal brings people of all backgrounds together. We hope you enjoy these delicious recipes, build community, and fight alongside us for a future where everyone is able to move freely. Building the world we dream of and deserve might start in the kitchen…

Thank you from all of us at CIRC!

ACKNOWLEDGMENTS

Writing this book has been a journey of growth, made brighter and more fun by the invaluable contributions of the following people:

Participants, who shared their time and stories with us, making this project possible. We will forever treasure each of you and your stories in our hearts.

Sarah Jackson, whose visionary perspective was instrumental in shaping the inception of this book, and whose existential inquiries continue to inspire us. Nope, we still don't know what the meaning of life is... but when we figure it out, you'll be the first to hear!

Dr. Bryan Rojas-Araúz, our friend and qualitative research expert. Your insights and partnership always push us to think critically and center social justice.

University of Denver Undergraduate and Graduate Students, who lent their talent to all aspects of creating this book. Madison Kim, Brigid Magdamo, Arleigh Perkins, Patricia Garcia, Hannah Branch, Akilah Martin, and Emily Leeper, your contributions have enriched our project immensely.

Maria del Carmen Giaggeri (Julia's Mom), for your unwavering support and your challenging us *a pensar más fuerte* (to think harder). Oh, yeah, and for babysitting while we poured our hearts into this roller coaster!

Domingo and Bherta Robles, who taught Julia, upon her arrival in the U.S., about the many challenges faced by undocumented immigrants. Your kindness and guidance make all the difference in the world!

Center for Community Engagement to Advance Scholarship & Learning (CCESL) at the University of Denver, for their faith in, patience with, and funding of our book. And special thanks to Dr. Cara DiEnno! Your support, and everything we have learned from you throughout the years, has been a driving force behind the success of this project.

Lorna Bonnell, a graduate of the Denver Publishing Institute (DU), for her insightful review of our work.

Germán Frers, our dear friend and editor, who generously volunteered his expertise. His guidance went far beyond just the technicalities of publishing, emphasizing the power of storytelling through both language and formatting.

Alana Goldberg, for her meticulous editing and invaluable contributions to refining our book. We don't know what we would have done without you!

There are many others not listed here who have also contributed their wisdom and support to this book and to our work in community, more generally—to them, many thanks! Your collective support and commitment have been indispensable, and we are deeply thankful for the collaborative spirit that has shaped this project.

With gratitude,

Julia & Delio

OUR
CONCEPT

Every year, hundreds of thousands of non-citizens in the U.S. find themselves detained by Immigration and Customs Enforcement (ICE) officials. In the shadows of these statistics lies a human toll that often goes untold. Our cookbook is born out of a desire to amplify the voices and stories of immigrants who have experienced the profound challenges of immigration and/or detention in the United States. We embarked on a mission to create a cookbook that goes beyond mere recipes.

Our cookbook is a platform for immigrants in our community to share both cherished recipes and the profound narratives of their immigration journeys, including encounters with detention.

Food has the power to nurture, connect, and evoke memories. We celebrate participants who shared their life stories while cooking and eating with us. Each recipe comes with a story, in first-person voice, an intimate glimpse into the lives of those who have faced unimaginable challenges in their immigration to the United States.

This cookbook is not just a celebration of diverse cuisines; it's a social justice initiative, reflecting our commitment to addressing the toll of immigration and detention. By bringing these stories to light, we aim to foster understanding, compassion, and solidarity.

NOURISH & EMPOWER

Theoretical Framework

JULIA RONCORONI

The theoretical underpinnings of this project are deeply rooted in the concepts of liberation psychology, community psychology, and radical healing, which collectively inform our approach to addressing the profound effects of immigration and displacement on individual and community health.

Liberation Psychology and Community Empowerment

Liberation psychology emphasizes a commitment to the transformation of society through understanding the socio-political dimensions of distress, particularly in the pursuit of justice for oppressed populations (Torres Rivera, 2020). In his foundational work on liberation psychology, Ignacio Martín-Baró (1994) discusses de-alienation as a subjective process where individuals reclaim fragmented historical pasts to reconstitute themselves and break free from an oppressive, alienating present. Baró invites us: "The task of the psychologist must be to achieve the de-alienation of groups and persons by helping them attain a critical understanding of themselves and their reality" (Baró, 1994, p.41). The "Cocina Libre" cookbook aims to empower marginalized immigrant communities, not only as subjects of scholarly interest but as agents of change and narrators of their own stories, in this way encouraging *de-alienation*. It shifts the focus from a traditional deficiency-oriented view of individual suffering to a broader context, recognizing the systemic injustices that contribute to the psychological trauma experienced by immigrants.

Both liberation psychology and community empowerment advocate for an empathetic engagement with the lived experiences of oppressed individuals, urging an understanding that these experiences are not isolated incidents but are deeply embedded in unjust power structures. By integrating these frameworks, our project does not merely document experiences but actively participates in the decolonization of knowledge, valuing the voices and stories of immigrants as fundamental to both community-based and scholarly discourses.

Radical Healing

Building on the foundations laid by liberation psychology and community empowerment, the concept of radical healing is central to our methodology. Radical healing (French et al., 2020) encompasses strategies that individuals and communities use to foster resilience and create a sense of wholeness in the face of social and systemic oppression. It is an act of resistance against dehumanizing experiences, such as those endured by immigrants. Radical

Theoretical Framework

CONT'D

healing entails addressing racial trauma, pursuing liberation and wholeness, and resisting oppressive conditions (Adames et al., 2022; French et al., 2020; Ginwright, 2010; Mosley et al., 2020).

In our project, cooking and sharing of meals serve as a medium for radical healing, transforming a simple act of eating into a powerful expression of cultural identity, community bonding, and mutual support. This not only helps mitigate the trauma associated with immigration and displacement but also reasserts the humanity and dignity of the participants. The stories shared over meals then become artifacts of this healing process, documenting the journey from isolation to community integration and empowerment.

Integration with Project Goals and Methods
By documenting the narratives and recipes of immigrants, we aim to produce more than a collection of stories; we are crafting a tool for community healing and social justice. The methodology of engaging immigrants in narrating their stories while sharing meals aligns with the principles of these frameworks. It ensures that the research process is participatory and grounded in the experiences and needs of the community. This approach not only enriches the data collected but also facilitates a therapeutic engagement for the participants, embodying the principles of radical healing by providing a space for reflection, empowerment, and resistance.

Theoretical Framework

CONT'D

Conclusion

This project is a deliberate effort to bridge academic research with community action, informed by a robust theoretical framework that emphasizes justice, empowerment, and healing. As Dominican-American writer Junot Diaz (2016) reminds us: "While we're doing the hard, necessary work of mourning, we should avail ourselves of the old formations that have seen us through darkness. We organize. We form solidarities. And, yes: we fight. To be heard. To be safe. To be free." By integrating the principles of liberation psychology, community empowerment, and radical healing, we aim to contribute to the scholarly discourse on immigration while simultaneously offering tangible benefits to the immigrant community through engagement, empathy, and the transformative power of shared narratives.

References:

Adames, H. Y., Chavez-Dueñas, N. Y., Lewis, J. A., Neville, H. A., French, B. H., Chen, G. A., & Mosley, D. V. (2022). Radical healing in psychotherapy: Addressing the wounds of racism-related stress and trauma. Psychotherapy. https://doi.org/10.1037/pst0000435

Diaz, J. (2016, November 14). Under President Trump, Radical Hope Is Our Best Weapon. The New Yorker. https://www.newyorker.com/magazine/2016/11/21/under-president-trump-radical-hope-is-our-best-weapon

French, B. H., Lewis, J. A., Mosley, D. V., Adames, H. Y., Chavez-Dueñas, N. Y., Chen, G. A., & Neville, H. A. (2020). Toward a Psychological Framework of Radical Healing in Communities of Color. The Counseling Psychologist, 48(1), 14–46. https://doi.org/10.1177/0011000019843506

Ginwright, S. A. (2010). Black youth rising: Activism and radical healing in urban America. Teachers College Press.

Mosley, D. V., Neville, H. A., Chavez-Dueñas, N. Y., Adames, H. Y., Lewis, J. A., & French, B. H. (2020). Radical hope in revolting times: Proposing a culturally relevant psychological framework. Social and Personality Psychology Compass, 14(1). https://doi.org/10.1111/spc3.12512

Torres Rivera, E. (2020). Concepts of liberation psychology. In L. Comas-Díaz & E. Torres Rivera (Eds.), Liberation psychology: Theory, method, practice, and social justice. (pp. 41–51). American Psychological Association. https://doi.org/10.1037/0000198-003

Convención, Perú

Ingrid Encalada Latorre

"I immigrated to the United States in the year 2000, when I was 17 years old. I had to leave my family because I was a teenager. It was very difficult for me. I left behind my siblings, my parents, seeking better opportunities in this country. When I arrived, it wasn't as easy as I had thought. I came undocumented, without a social security number. In 2002, I bought fake documents to be able to put food on the table, to sustain myself. In 2008, my first son, Bryan, was born. I was very excited to have my little one. In 2010, I was arrested by the local police for using fake documents. I was in jail for 90 days. My son stayed with my aunt. I felt abandoned in jail. They told me they were going to deport me without being able to fight my case. It's very difficult to be separated from your two-year-old son. I paid the IRS a lot of money, like $12,000, for using fake documents. I have been fighting my immigration case since that time. In 2016, my legal case was denied because I did not meet all the requirements. I had bad representation from lawyers. I made the decision to seek asylum in the church to reopen my federal case. Honestly, I didn't feel guilty. I was sheltered for five years in three different churches, with my children. They are always with me in my struggle."

Stuffed Peppers

INGREDIENTS

8 poblano peppers

1 ½ cups vegetable oil

1 lb ground beef

Salt, pepper, garlic to taste

1 white onion, chopped

1 lb. queso fresco (cheese)

9 eggs

1 ½ cups unbleached white flour

DIRECTIONS

1. Preheat oven to 500°F. Line the raw peppers on a baking sheet covered with foil.

2. Bake the peppers for about 45 minutes, until the skins are blackened and blistered, rotating occasionally. Once roasted, place the peppers in a plastic bag, to sweat them, for 1 hour. Once the peppers are cool to the touch, use a paring knife to scrape off as much charred skin as possible. You can also place the chiles under running water and rub the skin off with your fingers. This is faster, but you lose some roasted flavor. Remove seeds and veins from the peppers. Set aside to dry.

3. Heat 2 tbsp of vegetable oil. Cook ground beef until browned. Season with salt, pepper, and garlic powder. Add the chopped onion; continue cooking 7-8 minutes.

4. Chop the queso into tiny cubes (shredded cheese works too). Fill the peppers with cheese and the meat mixture. You can use toothpicks to close the peppers.

5. Heat the rest of the oil over high heat in a pan. It should be hot enough that a drop of batter will sizzle when dropped in the oil.

6. Beat 9 egg whites until they form stiff white peaks. Fold in the egg yolks.

7. Place flour, salt, and pepper (adobo works like magic here!) in a shallow bowl and coat each pepper in flour, one by one, dusting off the excess flour.

8. Dip peppers in egg mixture and fry until golden, around 5 minutes on each side.

Tip: Sub ground beef with meatless meat (i.e., textured soy) for vegetarian chiles.

Tetiana Stratilat

"Someone once told me that all that is important in life you can carry in your two hands, so I took my son and my cat, and we fled Kyiv in the early morning hours of February 24, 2022. The next six days I'll never forget in my whole life because we were without food and water, and the temperatures were in the single digits. Normally, the drive from Kyiv to the Polish border takes about six hours. It took us two days because the highways were being bombed. I slept very little, and I didn't know when we would find food, water, or fuel. I saw a woman carrying something hot, and I ran to her and asked her, "Lady, where did you buy food?" And she said, "I didn't buy it. The Military allowed my husband to bring us food." And I said, "Oh! Sorry!" And she asked me, "Are you hungry?" I said, "No, of course not." I then went back to our car, and I said to my son, "It's healthy to starve sometimes." But you know, humor did not help at that moment. The point of this story is that she knocked on our car window, and she shared her food with us. She shared her food despite not knowing when she would receive more food and how long she would be in the border queue. She had three children in her car, but she still shared. Her name was Nadiya, which means hope. So, when I tell people that food sustains and feeds us, I also say that food gives us hope. As a chef, I have tasted thousands of dishes, believe me, but the taste of that dish I will remember my whole life. It took us 66 hours to travel less than two miles to the Polish border, often waiting hours to be able to move forward just a few meters. But we did it! We spent a week in Poland, three months in Germany, and, in June, we arrived in the US."

Potato Vareniki

For the Dough:
8.5 oz flour
4 tbsp melted butter
1 egg, room temperature
3.7 oz warm whole milk
1/2 tsp salt

DIRECTIONS

1. Add flour, melted butter, egg, and salt into a food-processor bowl.

2. Turn the food processor on low speed and slowly add warm milk without stopping the processor until all ingredients are well incorporated. You can also do this manually. The dough should be smooth and not stick to your hands.

3. Transfer the dough to a double-zipper bag and let rest in the fridge overnight or until the dough is cool. The dough will stick a little, but after resting in the cold, it will be more elastic.

For Assembly:

2 lbs golden potatoes

1/4 gallon whole milk

Salt and pepper to taste

1 tsp sugar

1 head garlic

6 tbsp neutral oil

4-5 sprigs thyme

1 lb sweet white onion

1 recipe vareniki dough

8 slices bacon

DIRECTIONS

1. Peel potatoes, and cut them into ½ inch cubes. Bring them to a boil in cold milk, with salt. Set heat to medium low. Cook until soft. drain, and mash until smooth.

2. Preheat oven to 400°F. Slice the garlic head in half across the middle, and season with salt, pepper, 1 tbsp oil, and thyme. Bake wrapped in foil until golden (~30-40 min). When cool, squeeze cloves out of the head. Mash and add to the potatoes.

3. Preheat 3 tbsp oil in a large skillet. Peel and cube the onion. Add cubed onion to hot oil. Fry on high for 3-5 minutes. Add salt, pepper, and sugar. Reduce the heat to medium and cook, stirring often, for 3-5 minutes. Add 2-3 tbsp of water. Cook while water evaporates completely, then fry until onions are nicely caramelized. Mix mashed potatoes with 1/4 of the caramelized onions. Season with salt and pepper.

4. Take the dough out of the refrigerator, roll it into a log with a diameter of 1-1.5 inches on a floured surface, cut into equal pieces that are 1/2-3/4 inches thick. Cover the dough with plastic film, as it dries quickly. Roll out the pieces thinly, and place the filling in the middle of each round piece of dough. Fold the dough into a semicircle, pinch the edges to seal, and you'll end up with a crescent roll.

5. Boil about 1.5 gallons of water, add 1 tbsp of salt, and put 8-10 dumplings in. Stir gently, moving the spoon along the side of the pot so as not to damage the dumplings. When they float to the surface, continue to cook for another 5 minutes.

6. Cover a baking tray with foil, place the bacon in a single layer, and broil in the oven for 5 minutes or until the bacon is well cooked. Transfer the bacon to a paper towel to get rid of the grease. Cut the bacon into medium pieces.

7. Heat a non-stick frying pan with 2 tbsp oil. Fry the dumplings on both sides until lightly golden. Serve the dumplings sprinkled with caramelized onions and bacon, with a few spoonfuls of cold sour cream, and a sprinkling of chopped dill on the side. Смачного! (Enjoy!)

Sandra Lopez

"It's very unfair. What fault do I have for what my government does? I came because I wanted a better future. I came fleeing from many things. In Mexico, I was in Chihuahua. There, I was single, living with my parents. Later, I met my husband, and we came here.

I was 21 when I came, still young. I've spent almost my entire life here in the United States. I've missed out on a lot. I lost my mother and couldn't be there with her. Two days before my mother died, I talked to her on the phone. The lengths one will go! I had to apologize. 'Mother, forgive me, for I cannot be with you. Look at my problem. My situation does not allow me to be free.' Such is the love of a mother, truly, that they understand. They understand. She said, 'Don't worry, *m'ija*, you will one day be free. Fight, fight for your dreams.' And it's so hard to feel that this last breath is ending, that it's fading. That sigh from your mother is like a little candle that has its light and is fading away. I felt her voice was so tired. I felt it was the last time I would speak with my mother. And that's how it was."

Sandra Lopez

"I remember one night my husband and I were arguing. All couples argue, most of the time about silly things. It was something silly we were arguing about, about the TV. I wanted to watch a soap opera that I really loved. He wanted to watch another program. And so, the argument started. It wasn't even about something serious, something big. Our kids were in the room. The youngest had never heard us argue before. He got scared. Children are taught in school to dial 911 in an emergency. And he got scared. Being just a kid, the youngest ran out of his room, and he dialed. He only dialed 911 and hung up the phone. When my child did that, I was no longer in the living room or even arguing with my husband. My husband wasn't there either. Nothing, nothing. Nothing at all. He was in one place, and I was in another. So that's how it happened. He just dialed 911 and hung up.

Then, the police arrived. They knocked on the door. As soon as they found out I didn't have a Colorado ID, they arrested me and put handcuffs on me. The police officer started yelling at me really ugly. His behavior changed immediately. As we left, he yelled at me ugly, treated me badly, yelled at me ugly. Well, that was his intention. He locked me up. I was in jail. He took all my information and immediately turned me over to ICE. That same night they arrested me, around 12:30 at night, immigration called me on the phone. They called me, and then I spoke with them. That's how it was. I spent two weeks in jail because of what happened. Since there was no evidence that my husband had accused me or that I had accused my husband of domestic violence, they dropped the charges. Before they dropped the charges, they were calling my house, harassing my husband to accuse me of domestic violence and saying that they could help my husband. They were offering him something good, you know what. And my husband said, 'No, never. I will never accuse my wife in such a way just for that.' My husband spoke with the prosecutor and told him what they were doing, that they were harassing him to accuse me of domestic violence. It was so unfair. The prosecutor told him, 'Don't worry. I'm carefully reviewing your wife's case. Don't listen to them. Your wife is going to come out fine from all this. Unfortunately, she is already with immigration. And you know how the system is.' That's how it was. I had my court hearing. The judge said to me, 'I'm sorry this happened to you.' The judge apologized. He said, 'I wish you luck.' He already knew whose hands I was in next. And it has not been easy. It has been an 8-year struggle. I have paid more than $40,000 fighting my case, buying time in the United States. Do you think that's fair? Buying time! I don't even own my own time, or my freedom, nothing."

Guac & Bean Tostadas

INGREDIENTS

1 can (15.5oz) pinto beans

Adobo to taste

1/2 head romaine lettuce

2 Roma tomatoes

8 oz mushrooms

1/2 cup cilantro leaves

3 avocados

Salt and pepper to taste

1 lemon

1 cup vegetable oil

12 corn tortillas

12 oz shredded cheese

DIRECTIONS

1. Simmer beans, seasoned with adobo, for 5-7 minutes.

2. Julienne the lettuce. Thinly slice the tomatoes. Chop the mushrooms and cilantro.

3. Prepare guacamole: mash avocados with salt, pepper, and fresh lemon juice.

4. Heat 1 cup oil, test with a tostada; when it sizzles, fry tortillas until golden brown on both sides. Depending on the kitchen, this can take between 1 1/2-2 minutes on each side. The finished tostadas should have a light to medium brown color.

5. Carefully remove, using the tongs, and let them cool on a paper-towel-covered plate.

6. Repeat for the remaining tortillas.

7. Remove the softened beans from the stove. Drain. Finish mashing beans by hand or with a food processor.

8. Spread the beans on the tostadas. Add guacamole, mushrooms, shredded cheese, sliced tomatoes, lettuce, and chopped cilantro.

Armando Hernandez

"I work installing tile floors. Someone at work got mad at me because I told them not to walk on the floor that had just been installed. He called the police accusing me of assault. His boss and mine told the police that I was innocent and we could resolve this internally. But they arrested me without evidence. I spent 30 days in state prison, with a $50,000 bond. I was acquitted in court, but my case was transferred to ICE, who ordered my deportation in 2014. With support from a congressman, I was granted a month to attend my daughter's graduation and leave for Mexico. That month, I went into sanctuary for nine months. I received a letter from ICE saying that I was not a deportation priority. In 2017, my case was reopened, I was detained in GEO, and my deportation order was reactivated. Legislators introduced a private bill to protect me from deportation for two years (until March 2019). The pardon expired, and I don't have any legal protection. Now I am at risk of ICE coming for me. They have my address, they know where we live, and they can come for me whenever."

Serves 5

Meat Empanadas

INGREDIENTS

4 eggs
2 tbsp vegetable oil
1 1/2 large white onion
1 lb ground beef
Salt and pepper to taste
1/2 cup green olives, chopped
1 handful green onions, chopped
2ct Roma tomatoes, cut small
1/2 tbsp cumin
1 tbsp oregano
1 1/2 tbsp paprika
20 Goya empanada discs

DIRECTIONS

1. Boil 3 eggs for 5 minutes, then chop when cool.

2. Heat the oil in a pan, sauté chopped white onion on medium heat for 8 minutes.

3. When the onion is smooth and translucent, add the meat. Season with salt and pepper, and stir until cooked.

4. To the cooked meat, mix in chopped eggs, olives, tomato pieces, and chopped green onions. (The green onions can be cooked but they lose flavor).

5. Season the filling with cumin, oregano, and paprika.

6. Allow the filling to cool (around 2 hours).

7. Preheat oven to 400°F.

8. Spoon filling onto each empanada disc, fold, and seal. To make the traditional Argentinean 'repulgue," twist and fold the edges of the empanada with your fingers. You can also seal using a fork.

9. With the 4th egg, egg wash the empanadas for a shiny crust.

10. Bake for 20-25 minutes until golden. Serve alone or with a sauce.

Uman, Ukraine

Olena Rudenko

"The main reason why we are here, in the United States, is because of the war. For me, the main priority is to have a safe place for my kid. Since I didn't feel safe anymore in Ukraine, and I had a few situations in my life where I saw rockets over my head, and it was so scary... and I could see weapons, and all those kind of things... we knew we could not stay... It was a huge risk. Even now, I have family in Ukraine. That's hard to explain, but... Physically, I'm here, but my mind and my soul are there. My parents and my sister are still in Ukraine. However, it's not safe to stay there anymore. Honestly, we are planning to come back. I mean, I'm really appreciative that I can stay here, that I can work, I can make friends, I can continue my life. However, everything is put on hold, and I'm just waiting for when I can come back home. So we continue to speak Ukrainian in our family, cook Ukrainian recipes, and keep in touch with our families. Your mind is there, and you cannot stop. It's ok when you plan to move somewhere and kind of prepare. When you don't plan and you just have to leave everything that you had behind, it's very hard. I never thought I would be in this type of situation and need to leave urgently. They didn't give me a choice."

Borscht

INGREDIENTS

4 tbsp oil to fry

1 yellow onion, finely chopped

2 carrots, peeled and thinly sliced

3 medium beets, peeled & grated

3-4 Yukon potatoes, cut small

1 pound of pork or beef

1 gallon water

1 ½ cans tomato paste

1 can (14.5oz) diced tomatoes

Salt & black pepper to taste

1 red cabbage

Optional: dill, 1 cup sour cream

DIRECTIONS

1. Heat 2 tbsp oil in a pot. Sauté onion until translucent.

2. Add the sliced carrots, grated beets, and diced potatoes to the pot. Cook for about 5-7 minutes until slightly softened.

3. In a separate pan, heat the remaining 2 tbsp of oil over medium heat. Brown the pork or beef on all sides. Then, add it to the pot with the vegetables.

4. Pour in all the water, and bring the mixture to a boil. Reduce the heat to low and let it simmer for about 20-30 minutes, or until the vegetables are tender and the meat is cooked through.

5. Stir in the tomato paste and (drained) diced tomatoes. Season with salt and black pepper. Let the soup simmer for 10-15 more minutes.

6. Add the thinly sliced cabbage to the pot, and cook for another 5-7 minutes until the cabbage is softened.

7. Serve the borscht hot—optional: top with dill and a dollop of sour cream.

Yraima Ylarraza

"I left my country seeking a better life for my daughters. Among those things, education, which is very important, and the economy. We came through the 'green paths,' as they call them. Through the Darien. It wasn't easy, but we made it. We made it. I came alone with my daughters, my daughter's boyfriend, and two nieces. Practically all women. The only guide we had on the way was God. No one else. First God. On the way, in the jungle, we didn't see any dead bodies or any of that. But being there is a very horrible experience because it's a desperation not knowing if you're going to make it out or not. And at one point, my knee bothered me and swelled up. And I cried because I thought, 'I'm not going to make it out of here with my daughters.' And well, I clung so much, so much to God that when I arrived at a camp, I didn't feel pain anymore. I have always said that one has to put God first. First God. In all things one is going to do in life, God. And well, the desperation of seeing my daughters crying because they saw their mom who couldn't walk and couldn't move forward. And I clung so much to God that I said, 'I have to get out for them.' Because I came for them."

Yraima Ylarraza

"We took a bus to *El Basurero*.* *El Basurero* is where we catch the train. I don't know if it was us Venezuelans who named it that, or if it was the people from Mexico, but it's called *El Basurero*. In *El Basurero*, there is... In each country, there's a spot for us migrants, like a refuge. There was a refuge there, near *El Basurero*. We arrived around six in the evening. What we did was buy 100 loaves of bread, liters of water, mayonnaise, sauce, tuna, cookies, and bread to get on the train, better known as *La Bestia*.

When they call it *La Bestia*, it's because it's horrible. It's horrible because... you don't know if it's going to stop, not going to stop. You're like waiting on... on the edge of the...

rails. When I say *La Bestia*, it's because some come very fast, they go very strong. I don't know, but on the train I was on, I had to go on top, in a well-closed wagon, where if we sit or stand, me being short, I see nothing, absolutely nothing. But I am safe there because I'm inside. There are some people who ride in other parts that are very dangerous. It really is very dangerous. And I thanked God at that moment, that that train was as if... as if guided by God. I was saying: 'And this is *La Bestia*? This is *La Bestia*?' Another guy told me: 'Ah, then you haven't been on... There are some that really go fast. There are some that... this and that'. And I said: 'We are blessed, we are blessed. We are fine, we are fine, we are fine'.

Well, it turns out that at night, they have to make a stop for an hour or two. We were in the middle of the desert, without knowing who is in the desert, who might get on the train, who might shoot. It's something very, very, very, very tough. That's why when they say that Mexico is worse than the jungle, yes, it is. Because in the jungle, you fall, you die, and that's it. Do you get it? But to be parked on the... on the train and for them to come and kidnap you, or take one of your daughters, or shoot one of your relatives... It's tough."

Basurero = spanish for garbage dump

Plantain Sandwich

INGREDIENTS

1 1/2 cup white cabbage, shredded

1 cup white vinegar

1 yellow onion, diced

3 cloves of garlic

16 oz ground beef

3 medium green plantains

2 cups oil, for frying

2 medium carrots, shredded

Mayo to taste

2 Roma tomatoes, diced

Ketchup to taste

DIRECTIONS

1. Soak cabbage in 1 cup of white vinegar for an hour. While you wait, go to the next step.

2. For the meat: In a large skillet, sauté diced onion and chopped garlic over medium-low heat until onions are translucent. Add ground beef and cook. Add the tomatoes. Stir and cook over low heat for 5 minutes until the flavors meld.

3. For the plantains: Peel and slice green plantains diagonally. Fry the slices in batches until golden brown. Remove and flatten each slice. In the same oil, fry the flattened plantain discs until crisp. Drain on paper towels.

4. Assembling the plantain sandwiches (patacones): Mix the cabbage with the carrots. Add mayo and salt to taste. Add a layer of cabbage and carrot on the bottom slice of a crisp plantain. Add the meat on top. Add ketchup to taste. Close the patacón with another plantain slice.

Tip: You can use meatless crumbles instead of ground beef.

Sandra Arellano

"I believe in destiny. I didn't plan to come here. I had my life and two children in Juarez. My husband came here first, on a visa. He is a welder and came here for a brief project. When I came to visit him, also on a visa, I was 7 months pregnant with my twins. He convinced me to give birth here. I wasn't planning on it—I had my doctor and hospital in Juarez. But he convinced me. We've been here for 17 years. Each person in our family has different status. My twins are citizens, my oldest children have DACA, and we are undocumented. We can't find a way to get us all on the same page."

Chicken Mole

INGREDIENTS

1 chicken, cut into 6 pieces

6 tbsp vegetable oil

1/4 cup whole almonds

1/2 cup sesame seeds

1 2.7 oz disk Mexican chocolate, chopped

4 dried ancho chiles, stemmed & seeded

6 dried Guajillo chiles, stemmed and seeded

3 cloves garlic, minced

1/4 tsp ground cinnamon

4 whole cloves

1/4 tsp ground coriander

1/4 tsp ground cumin

Black pepper to taste

Salt to taste

Chicken or vegetable broth

1/4 cup raisins

1 1/4 tbsp honey

Chicken Mole

DIRECTIONS

1. Add chicken, salt, and pepper with water to a pot (add enough water to cover the chicken in the pot). Simmer gently for about 40 minutes until the chicken is tender. Transfer chicken to a plate, and set aside the liquid.

2. Toast the almonds and sesame seeds in a dry skillet, over medium heat, until golden brown, stirring frequently (~5 minutes).

3. Heat 4 tbsp of oil in the skillet over medium heat. Fry the chiles until lightly toasted (~2 minutes), then transfer to a bowl, cover with hot water, and soak until pliable (~30 minutes).

4. In a blender, combine the toasted almonds and sesame seeds (save 2 tbsp for garnish), toasted chilies, minced garlic, ground cinnamon, ground cloves, ground coriander, ground cumin, black pepper, and salt to taste. Blend until you have a smooth paste.

5. In the same skillet used for toasting the almonds and sesame seeds, heat the chili paste over medium heat for 2-3 minutes, stirring constantly.

6. Gradually add the chicken or vegetable broth, raisins, chopped chocolate, and honey. Stir until the chocolate is melted and the sauce is well combined.

7. Simmer the mole sauce over low heat for about 15-20 minutes, stirring occasionally, until it thickens.

8. Taste and adjust the seasoning if needed. If the sauce is too thick, you can add more broth to reach your desired consistency.

Chihuahua, Mexico

Victor Galván

"The kitchen is a place that is symbolic of my mother's teachings. When I was little, my mother (who raised me as a single mother) sold burritos for a living. I would look at the burritos and say, 'We are not going to sell as many.' And she would say, 'Just wait until the end of the day. We won't have any left.' She taught me persistence."

"I was denied a scholarship because I did not qualify for the College Opportunity Fund. I told them, 'Texas has it. We can have it.' The next session they'd revised it... and in May 2013, I stood behind the governor [Hickenlooper] who signed this bill. That day, the world changed. Everything that I had learned from my mom, my teachers, the leaders at the organization materialized. All of the struggle, all of the effort, and finally we could see something real, something that I helped create. It was an honor to be there and be a part of history for all undocumented students in Colorado. This is the reason why I do this work."

"My mother taught me that you not only cook for yourself but to share with your family, with the people you love. You always cook with love, always. That's organizing for me. You don't do it only for you, but to share. That's the reason why I do what I do."

Victor Galván

"I wasn't part of the decision [for my family to immigrate to the United States]. I was just *carry-on*. I was eight months old when we arrived. I came with my mom, my dad, and my older brother. In 1991. Really, it was for economic reasons. More recently, I've told people that I am an economic migrant, an economic refugee. Life in Mexico, in Chihuahua, at that time was not suitable for creating the life my parents wanted for me and my brother. So they came here to the United States. My dad had come several times and told my mom about it. And they decided to come. Several of my dad's siblings had already become residents. And he saw that we had the opportunity here to get educated, have a career. And so, we took the chance. They brought me and my brother. That's why we came.

My family was looking for a chance to have a house, a future, right, where my brother and I had opportunities. Yeah, it really was the opportunity. And well, Colorado is 16 hours from my town so it wasn't too difficult for them to get here. And we had family here. My dad saw that it was a great opportunity for us.

It wasn't so easy for my dad. He got very frustrated. In fact, he left about three years later. He left my mom a single mother with me and my brother. We were alone for a long time. My mom really was the rock, the foundation of our family. But it was difficult. And I believe that since the reform in 1986, there hasn't been much relief for immigrants in this country until more recently. And it's still very tough. But yes, at least Denver, Colorado, gave us a chance to get educated. And I found a way to support myself politically, and I did it."

Shrimp Ceviche

INGREDIENTS

2 lbs deveined shrimp

1 yellow onion, minced

10 limes

2 cucumbers

4 Roma tomatoes

2 jalapeños

1 young coconut

1 can coconut cream

Salt and pepper to taste

1 bag tostadas

Hot sauce to serve

DIRECTIONS

1. Chop the shrimp into 1/2-inch pieces. Mix the shrimp, finely chopped onion, and lime juice. Marinate in the refrigerator for 1 hour.

2. Finely dice the cucumber and tomatoes. Mince the jalapeño.

3. Open the coconut, discard the water or save it for a drink (it is not used in the ceviche), and separate the coconut flesh from the shell.

4. After the marination, add the diced tomatoes, cucumbers, minced onion, and minced jalapeños into the shrimp mixture. Add the coconut flesh and a can of coconut cream to the mixture.

5. Season with salt and pepper to taste.

6. Serve the ceviche with tostadas. Add hot sauce for extra kick.

Gladis Ibarra

"My destiny was always meant to be this, to work and meet many people. And not necessarily in immigrant rights... But I think that my experiences and above all... the simple fact of the people I work with every day, in the community, they are like my family. When I started this job, since DACA had been taken away, I wanted to learn how to defend myself, how to defend my family, how to stay united literally, in the same home. And very soon I realized that all the people who called our office asking for some kind of guidance or with a simple question... inevitably, they are my family because in each person of any age, I see my mom, or I see my dad, or I see my sisters.

When DACA was removed in September 2017, they gave a deadline for people who had a permit expiring before March 20 to renew it. And my sister's permit was expiring a day or two later. I remember we went to a workshop at MSU, where they were helping with the application and they were helping with scholarships. And they helped my sister. She filled out her whole application, and when she got to the revision point, they told her she did not qualify because her permit expired later. Then I remember that we left there, my two sisters and I, crying, the three of us, because we did not know what we were going to do because there were no more options. So there… those were the facts: you do not qualify, your permit is going to expire, you have to leave your employment, you cannot go to school anymore. For me, it was very hard to see how my sister's options ended. My heart broke.

The other day, I was talking with these girls, they told me that this was happening to them. Their DACA is going to expire, and they don't have money for the renewal. I told them, "I can help you." It's little things like these that, for me, are easy to do but change the lives of others. Just like it changed my parents' lives to have a driver's license and changed my sisters' lives to go to a workshop to renew their DACA, now I can be a part of that. I am a witness, living proof that we are changing lives. The people I work with and the people who have taught me are the change we want to see in this community. I think that my whole life was preparing me for today, for where I am right now."

Shrimp Empanadas

INGREDIENTS

For the dough:

2 cups Maseca white corn flour

2 cups water

1 tbsp salt

1 tbsp Huichol sauce

2 tsp baking powder

For the filling:

1 lb shrimp

2 Roma tomatoes

1/2 white onion

Salt and pepper to taste

2 tbsp vegetable oil

For the sauce:

1 large jalapeño, w/o stem & seeded

1 avocado

4 cilantro branches

2 limes

Salt and pepper to taste

1/4 cup water

Shrimp Empanadas

DIRECTIONS

1. To prepare the dough: mix the masa flour with the warm water, salt, Huichol sauce, and baking powder. Knead into a cohesive dough (until smooth). You want a moist masa that does not stick to your hands. Let the masa sit for 15 minutes. Tip: There is some trial and error in this step (based on your climate). If the dough is too dry, add 1 or 2 tbsp of water; if the dough is too wet, add flour.

2. Chop the shrimp into small, bite-size pieces. Season with salt and pepper to taste. Then, chop the tomato and the onion. Combine in a bowl with the shrimp.

3. Heat 2 tbsp oil over medium heat in a large frying pan. Add the shrimp, tomatoes, and onions. Cook the shrimp until they turn pink, about 3-5 minutes. Do not overcook the shrimp because they will become rubbery.

4. Remove pan from the heat, and let the filling cool before stuffing the empanadas.

5. Separate the dough into 20 golf-ball-sized chunks, rolling between the hands to form smooth balls. Cover so that they do not dry.

6. Wet your hands slightly. Place a ball of dough between your palms. Pat your hands together repeatedly and consistently, until a round tortilla emerges (pat-pat-pat method). You can also use a tortilla press for this step.

7. Place a spoonful of filling in the center of the tortilla (empanada dough). Fold the dough in a half-circle shape, and seal the edges (by hand or with a fork). If the edges are not well sealed, the empanada will burst and you will lose filling when frying them.

8. Fry the filled empanadas at 375°F for 3-4 minutes per side. They should be lightly golden. Drain on paper towels. Cool slightly before serving.

9. For the sauce: In a blender, put the jalapeño, avocado pulp, cilantro branches, juice from the lime, and 1/4 cup of water. Blend until smooth.

10. Serve the empanadas with the sauce.

Puebla, México

Laura Peniche

"[Crossing the border] was hard but not that hard. I think we were very lucky. We tried to cross once and walked a lot, like through rough terrain. We got lost. We were caught and sent back. But, that time we were caught, we met a young man who said he lived at the border and he said he would teach us how to cross back to the United States. He said he'd been deported nine times. But he said, 'I live on this side of the river, so I will always come back.' He lived crossing the river, in a community of mobile homes. Then that's the good luck we had. It was easy to cross. It was just crossing the river. It wasn't dangerous. We had to go through the checkpoint, the checkpoint in Texas. Then we had to walk again. We walked around the mountains. That was the hardest because we walked like six hours at night. My dad walked with his feet bleeding from the thorns, carrying my two little siblings. That memory has stayed with me. It is the sacrifice one makes as an immigrant because we have faith that we will find something better on the other side.

Coming here, we still have our innocence. We are not aware of how the immigration laws work in the United States. So we come with that innocence, with the hope that here we will be able to fix our papers. And once here, we are surprised.

Laura Peniche

"It's not very fair that immigrants and refugees are punished so severely knowing that those of us coming from other countries have no knowledge of how the laws work here. We don't even imagine that we could end up in detention and be locked up for so long. But I don't know. I'm always grateful to God because despite it being difficult, we have encountered many very kind people. From that guy who helped us cross, there are always more people who want to help than people who don't want to help. Many people with good hearts have helped us a lot.

It's hard to wake up to reality. Even though I grew up undocumented, I didn't have the need to go out to the community. I was scared. And I didn't feel there was something I could do that could change things. In fact, when I was invited, I never agreed to do things like tell my story and all of that. When the president won in 2016, it gave me… it made me really scared and disappointed in what I was seeing. My first instinct was to get out of here, out of this country, because I did not feel safe. And I wanted to leave. I wanted to go to Mexico or anywhere, somewhere else. But at the same time, it's not easy to leave because if I have children here, and their father lives here, how are you going to separate them from their father? Their father is from here. Those are things that most people don't understand. Sometimes one feels trapped here. So seeing that… That's what gave me the most despair, knowing that, even if I want to leave, I can't leave. That's what gave me the determination to rather go out and work in the community, seek ways to raise awareness among people at least, try to join efforts to change the laws. And that helped me a lot. It helped me feel better, to feel that I wasn't alone."

Serves 6

Green Chilaquiles

INGREDIENTS

1 tbsp minced garlic

3 jalapeños

12 tomatillos

1 large red or yellow onion

1 handful cilantro

2 avocados

12 corn tortillas

1 cup vegetable oil, for frying

Salt and pepper to taste

1 cup sour cream

1 cup queso fresco

DIRECTIONS

1. Make salsa verde (i.e., green sauce): Peel and chop garlic. Seed and mince the jalapeños. Bring tomatillos to a boil in a medium sauce pan, barely covering them with water. Reduce heat to medium-low, and add chiles and garlic until soft (~12-15 mins). Let cool.

2. Drain the tomatillos, reserving 1/2 cup of cooking liquid.

3. Blend tomatillos, chiles, and garlic with 1/2 cup cooking liquid, leaving some texture.

4. Chop the onion and cilantro. Slice the avocado into wedges.

5. Cut tortillas into 6 wedges each.

6. Fry the tortilla chips in batches until golden (~2-3 minutes). Transfer to a paper-towel-lined plate to cool. Season with salt. Repeat batches. Tip: for a healthier option, tortillas can be air fried or baked in the oven.

7. In the saucepan, simmer salsa verde until thickened (~5 minutes). Then add fried tortilla chips, coat, and season with salt and pepper, as needed.

8. Serve on a plate immediately to ensure that the tortilla chips remain crispy. Garnish with chopped onion, sour cream, grated queso fresco, a slice or two of avocado, and chopped cilantro. You can use any topping you like, including sliced or diced radishes, pickled red onions, chopped jalapeños, etc.

Angélica Crespo

"The journey was very tough. It took us two months and 10 days to arrive here. The jungle was really tough. We spent three and a half days in the Darien jungle. After getting out, we reached Panama. In Panama, it was difficult to leave the UN camp because we had to pay for transportation, and we didn't have money. There was a lot of extortion to get through the jungle. They take too much money. But well, thank God, we managed to get out of there. We did well in Costa Rica. Many people helped us by giving us work. They also donated money to us. There, we managed to gather enough to keep moving forward. We arrived in Nicaragua. Nicaragua was the easiest. We crossed it super quickly. The same day we arrived, we left. Honduras wasn't as tough either. We spent like three or four days in Honduras. After that, we left. Guatemala was a bit difficult. A lot of extortion from the police on the road. We were traveling in a minibus. The police, every 20 or 30 minutes, would stop the minibus to extort, to extort, to extort. And it was very tough because they were leaving us with no money. Mexico was... another jungle. As they say, the concrete jungle. It was very tough. A lot of extortion. The transporters, immigration, police... No, that was very tough. We spent many days in Mexico. Walking... We walked a lot, a lot. We cried, laughed, fought... It was a relief to arrive here."

Angélica Crespo

"In the Darien, there are different routes to enter the jungle. There are Acandí, Carreto, and Capurganá. Carreto is the most expensive because it's the easiest to cross. It can be crossed in a day or a day and a half. Acandí is a bit less expensive and takes two days, though some people take up to a week. My partner and I entered through Capurganá. It is the least expensive, the cheapest. It took us three and a half days to get out of Capurganá, out of the jungle. It's very difficult because... On the first day, we reached La Bandera, which is already the border of Colombia and Panama. We left La Bandera and arrived at a place where there is a mountain. I don't remember if they call it La Llorona or La Montaña de la Muerte. I don't know which of the two it is. And there we had to camp because we couldn't move forward after five in the evening. It's very dangerous. There, many people camped, in tents. There is a lot of trash in that place. As best we could, we laid down cardboard and clothes that had been discarded to rest better. At seven in the morning the next day, we began to climb the mountain. One has to climb almost lying down. There is a lot of mud. The mountain has a lot of mud. It's very difficult to climb. There are people who slip because it is too steep. The mountain takes about four hours to climb up and down. It took us about two and a half hours, going up and down. The descent is super difficult. It's very slippery. At least, I almost fell down a ravine while going down. If it weren't for one of the guys with us, who grabbed my arm, I wouldn't be here telling my experience. I wouldn't be here.

We managed to get down the mountain. We arrived to walk downstream to continue. That same day we had to camp near a river. Around twelve or one in the

morning, it began to rain. The rivers rose. We had to climb up a mountain because the water was reaching us. In the morning, we woke up, took down the tents, and arrived at a place where the Panamanian military were. They told us that we couldn't cross the river because it was too rough. The river had a rope where people would pass and hold on. But the current was very strong below and would lift people up, and if they didn't hold on, it would carry them away.

Arepas with Egg

INGREDIENTS

2 cups white corn flour, precooked
1/2 tsp salt
1 1/2 cups warm water
1/2 cup cooking oil
4 boiled eggs
2 avocados
Mayonnaise to taste

DIRECTIONS

1. In a bowl, mix the precooked corn flour with the salt.

2. Add water little by little, mixing well to avoid lumps, until you have a smooth dough. Let the dough rest for 5-10 minutes.

3. Form the dough into balls, and flatten them with your hands to form discs.

4. Coat a frying pan with a thin layer of oil. Heat over medium heat.

5. Cook the arepas in the hot skillet, turning occasionally, until golden brown on both sides.

6. While the arepas are cooking, peel the boiled eggs and cut them into thin slices. Cut the avocado into wedges.

7. Once the arepas are ready, cut them in half and spread mayonnaise inside.

8. Add salt to the slices of boiled eggs. Place them in the arepa. Add the avocado. Close the arepa.

And there you have it! Now you can enjoy a delicious arepa with boiled egg, avocado, and mayonnaise. Enjoy your meal!

Arepas with Black Beans

INGREDIENTS

2 cups white corn flour, precooked

1 tsp salt

1 1/2 cups warm water

1/2 cup cooking oil

1 can black beans, drained & rinsed

DIRECTIONS

1. In a large bowl, mix the precooked corn flour with salt. Gradually add warm water, and mix until you have a smooth dough. Let the dough rest for 5-10 minutes.

2. Divide the dough into portions, and shape them into walnut-sized balls. Then, flatten each ball to form the arepas, making sure they have a uniform thickness.

3. Coat a frying pan with a thin layer of oil. Heat over medium heat. Cook the arepas for about 5-7 minutes on each side or until they are golden brown and fully cooked.

4. While the arepas are cooking, you can prepare the black beans. In a pan, heat the cooked black beans, and mash them slightly with a fork. Season them with salt and spices of choice (e.g., cumin, adobo, chili powder, or garlic powder) to taste.

5. Once the arepas are ready, cut them in half, and add the black beans. You can season with salt and pepper to taste. Serve while warm.

Enjoy!

Tip: You can also add avocado and/or cheese to your black bean arepas.

Guadalajara Mexico
Alejandro Flores

As immigrants, the only thing we can do in terms of money or work is to start businesses. It's the only thing you can do: food. When I was a kid, one of the things my mom sold was cheesecakes and flans. She went door to door selling them. This was after her regular job. And much of our community does that, sells tamales or sells food. Or they know how to do something and that's how they start their business. But they can never get out of running a small business. It's always about who you know. "Oh, I know this person who knows how to make tacos" or "I know this person who knows how to make this type of food." And they just grab contracts for that, or only during the holidays.

What I want is to expand our food businesses, from cooking only in our kitchens to cooking in a restaurant. Having customers and a business with employees and all that. Small businesses. I recognize that many times this lives in our community, being entrepreneurs, but we don't know it. We think in terms of surviving, of putting food on the table, not of getting rich and leaving an inheritance. It's more like "What do I have to do to pay the rent? What do I have to do to buy books for school?" I want to reach a point where I can leave this for my community.

I want to be able to buy the building so I don't have to rent anymore. The building will be mine. And I can choose who lives there. And my tenants will look like me. My tenants will live the experiences I have lived. My tenants will be my community. I've heard the term "gentification." Not gentrification, GENTIFICATION. A return. People like me who grew up in these neighborhoods are now going to come back educated. They went to fuckin' Berkeley, Harvard, all these places. And now they're going to come back with an education to the community. For me, it's a bit different. I'm going to come back with a business. I didn't go the education route. I wasn't in a classroom learning about business, SEO, social media, etc. I learned by doing. And now I'm going back to the community. That's my job. It's my motivation."

Poke Bowl

INGREDIENTS

For the Salmon Poke:
2 tbsp soy sauce
1 tbsp sesame oil
1 tsp rice vinegar
1 tsp honey or maple syrup
1/2 tsp grated fresh ginger
1/2 tsp chopped green onions
1/2 tsp sesame seeds
1 lb sushi-grade salmon
For the Guacamole:
2 ripe avocados, peeled & pitted
1 lime
1/4 cup finely chopped red onion
1/4 cup chopped fresh cilantro
Salt and pepper to taste
For assembly:
3 cups cooked & cooled sushi rice
1 tbsp Sriracha mayonnaise
2 tbsp sesame seeds

DIRECTIONS

1. Combine soy sauce, sesame oil, rice vinegar, honey or maple syrup, grated ginger, chopped green onions, and sesame seeds in a bowl. Cube the salmon and add it to the marinade, gently toss to coat, and refrigerate for 30 minutes.

2. In another bowl, mash ripe avocados with a fork. Add lime juice, chopped red onion, cilantro, salt, and pepper. Mix until creamy, seasoning to taste.

3. Distribute rice evenly among bowls.

4. Drain excess marinade from the salmon. Place salmon cubes on top of the rice in each bowl.

5. Spoon a generous dollop of guacamole beside the salmon.

6. Drizzle spicy Sriracha mayo over the salmon and guacamole, adjusting to taste. Decorate with sesame seeds.

Afsanah Noori

"We just got here two years ago. My husband was an interpreter for the United States. When the Taliban took over Afghanistan, my husband's life wasn't very safe, so that's why we got here. We were six months in the camps, in the U.S. army camps. Then, after that, they sent us to Colorado because we have some friends here. Yeah, that's why we got here. You know, the Taliban don't like the people working with the United States, so they're gonna kill everybody who works with the United States. And my husband was working with the United States army. He was an interpreter, so there wasn't a safe place for him. When the Taliban took over Afghanistan, they were looking for my husband. And my husband just escaped from one place to another place to save his life. We left Afghanistan in August '21, and we were six months in different army camps. By that point, I had my son. He was just two and a half. Yeah. almost three. He was almost three when we left Afghanistan. Actually, it was very hard for me because we left everything over there and we left Afghanistan with just two backpacks. So, from other side, I was very happy because my husband was safe and, from other side, I was very sad because of my family. I left my family who were there in Afghanistan, but right now the situation in Afghanistan is not very good. Most of the people there are jobless. Everything is very, very expensive over there, and actually it's very hard for me and my husband to be in this situation. But I'm happy for my family here. All the schools in Afghanistan are shut down for ladies, for women, yeah. So, at least here my daughter can go to school, and I can continue my education too, here. And my son and husband are safe here."

Kotlat Kachaloo

INGREDIENTS

5 Yukon gold potatoes

1 yellow onion

1/4 cup oil, for frying

1 tsp salt

1 tsp turmeric

1 tsp curry powder

1 tsp black pepper

DIRECTIONS

1. Peel the potatoes and cut them into chunks. Place the chunks in a large pot and cover them with water. Bring the water to a boil over medium-high heat and cook the potatoes until they are fork-tender, about 15-20 minutes.

2. While the potatoes are cooking, peel and finely chop the yellow onion.

3. In a separate pan, heat 3 tbsp of oil over medium heat. Add the chopped onion and sauté until it turns golden brown and caramelized, about 5-7 minutes.

4. Once the potatoes are cooked, drain them and transfer them to a large mixing bowl. Mash the potatoes using a potato masher until smooth and lump-free.

5. Add the sautéed onion to the mashed potatoes. Add the salt, turmeric, curry powder, and black pepper to the mashed potatoes and mix well until the spices are evenly incorporated. Taste and adjust the seasoning if necessary.

6. Divide the mashed potato mixture into equal portions and shape them into round potato pancakes or patties.

7. Heat the rest of the oil in a frying pan over medium heat. Once it is hot, carefully place the pancakes in the pan. Fry the pancakes until they are golden brown and crispy on both sides, about 3-4 minutes per side. Once done, remove the potato pancakes from the pan and drain them on paper towels to remove excess oil.

Durango, Mexico

Homero Ocón

"I came to Denver in 1999, in January. I come from Mexico, from Durango, in the north-central part of Mexico. I came here hoping to have a better life. And no, rather, many people were coming at that time. And I felt that I couldn't stay there because there were no jobs and such. So, I arrived by bus. I crossed through Juarez and arrived here by bus at 7 in the morning on January 11, 1999. And I felt very happy. Even though I was leaving my entire family behind. In fact, I didn't think about the implications of coming like this at that time. And now I have my son and my wife and it's... The immigration laws are strict. I don't have, at this moment, the possibility to fix my papers unless I leave the country for 10 months to a year and a half. I'm thinking about the consequences of doing this because I have my young son, I have my marriage, and we have our house. I'm rather waiting for the law to change a bit, to make it possible for me to arrange my documents without leaving the country. Or another less difficult way, with fewer consequences for my son, and me, and my family. I have a small business painting houses. I have many clients. So, I would lose all of that. But at the same time, I have my family that I haven't seen in 20 years... nieces, sisters... I've seen some but not all. My parents used to come regularly since my sister, who was a year older than me, died. They arranged their visa and came, but now they can no longer do so."

"My father is almost 80 years old, and my mom is 72. It's harder for them to come here. I miss them so much. They live alone in a community that hardly has any people left. I feel a deep longing to go back there and support them, visit them, hug them... It's been 4 years since they last came. And that's it. There's a feeling of helplessness about why all this happened, why I got myself into this if I have friends who are there and are living well, or others who have already fixed their papers and are at peace. Now, I'm analyzing the effects of all the decisions I made when I was younger."

Tamales

INGREDIENTS

For the dough:

6 tbsp butter

1 cup cream cheese, room temp

4 cups Maseca corn flour

2 tsp baking powder

2 tbsp salt

1 tbsp ground pepper

1 tbsp garlic powder

4 cups veggie or chicken broth

For the filling:

8 poblano chiles

2 lbs queso fresco

16 dried corn husks

DIRECTIONS

1. Preheat the oven to 500°F. Place poblano chiles on a tray and roast for 40 minutes, turning every 10 minutes to ensure even roasting.

2. While the chiles are roasting, soak the dried corn husks in warm water for at least 30 minutes to make them pliable.

3. Mix butter and cream cheese until fluffy. Combine corn flour, baking powder, salt, pepper, and garlic powder. Slowly add the broth. Achieve a firm but soft dough.

4. Place roasted hot chiles in a sealed plastic bag to help separate the skin. Peel, remove seeds and stem, then cut into strips. Once cool, cut them into strips.

5. Prepare the filling by mixing the roasted poblano strips with the cheese and seasoning to taste with salt, pepper, and any desired spices.

6. Spread a soaked corn husk and place 2 tbsp of dough in the center. Spread. Add a spoonful of filling on top of the dough. Hold the husk vertically, with the narrow tip facing upwards. Leave 2 inches from the edges without dough. Fold into a cocoon, and wrap with the husk. Fold up the bottom.

7. Steam in a tamale maker or steamer for 50 minutes, or until the dough is firm and pulls away from the husk easily.

Gloria Durán

"When I thought about coming to the United States, I did it out of necessity. To help my family. When I came over here, I came without money. I didn't have money to come here. From Mexico City to here, I came on a trailer. Hitchhiking. I'd catch one trailer, then another, until I reached the border. I came with a friend, and we didn't have any money. We reached the border and went to a restaurant to ask for a job, to work and see if we could cross to the U.S. with some money. In that restaurant, it seemed very strange to us that [no one ever came in]. This was in Monterrey. When we asked for a job, we also asked if they had somewhere for us to stay because we didn't have a place to stay or money for a hotel. They told us we could stay at the restaurant because they had rooms separate from the restaurant. So, we stayed there. When we

finished at the restaurant, we went to sleep. The next day, when we woke up, we tried to leave the room, but we couldn't get out. We were locked in. There was a door to a little patio, but the wall was very, very high. So, no one could get out because the wall was too high. When we were outside, a girl came out crying, running. She screamed and cried. When we heard her, we ran to see what was going on. And then she said, 'No, ladies, don't leave. If you leave, I am going to be beaten.' When the girl said that, we got scared. We thought that the people who had given us a chance to stay might want to do something to us. It seemed weird that they locked the door, and the girl had stayed back to watch us and didn't want to let us go. Because of her reaction, we thought they might do something to us. My friend said, 'Let's lie down and pretend we are asleep so that the girl falls back asleep.' We pretended we were asleep, and the girl fell asleep. When she fell asleep, we got out. To jump the fence, which was really high, we climbed a tree that was really high. We said, 'When we get to the other side, we'll take the first car we see, to get out of here.'"

Gloria Durán

"We were headed for Piedras Negras. Over there in Piedras Negras, people were waiting for us to... to help us cross over here. So, when we crossed, we were going to walk for eight days through the desert. So, when we were on our way, we had passed like two fences because there are many fences to cross over here. There are quite a few fences.

So, when we were passing the second fence, one of the border patrol agents was looking down. When we... There were about 35 of us coming. So when we... when we saw that the border patrol was coming and they were focusing from above... they were in a helicopter and they were focusing... well, we all started running and hiding in all the bushes, or grass, I don't know what they're called. We hid. I jumped and when I jumped... I was pregnant with my daughter, the one who was born here. I was pregnant with her. And I also brought another lady besides my friend. So I jumped and, when I jumped, I fell into... there were a lot of thorns and I got a thorn stuck in my hand.

So when the helicopter passed, we... we got up. And what was our surprise? When we got up and looked for the 35 people who were with us, there wasn't a single person left. Only three of us remained. And that's because the person who was... that I brought from where I'm from... when she jumped and saw the helicopter, she fell. And everyone who was coming ran her over and injured her foot. So she couldn't walk. So when she got up, we couldn't run with the others. The three of us stayed and the other 32 disappeared. The lady I had brought with me stayed and another guy stayed.

The guy tells me: 'You know what? Let's go back. Because you two are women, and I'm a man. If someone sees us, maybe wanting to take advantage of you, they might hit me or something." So, since I was pregnant, I told the man: "Look, if you want to go back, OK, go back. But I'm already here. I'm not going back, I'm going to keep going until..." He says, 'How far are you going to keep going?' I said: 'As far as I can go."

Vegetable Stew

INGREDIENTS

For the vegetables:

8 medium carrots
3 medium potatoes

For the base of the sauce:

1 yellow onion
5 garlic cloves
6 Roma tomatoes
1/2 tsp pepper
1 tbsp mustard
1 tsp ground cumin
1/2 cup water
2 bouillon cubes

For the preparation:

2 cups olive oil

For the rice:

2 garlic cloves
1 yellow onion
1 red bell pepper
1 yellow bell pepper
2 cups rice
4 cups water
1 bouillon cube
Salt to taste

For the final sauce:

1/2 cup olive oil
1/2 red bell pepper
1/2 green bell pepper
1/2 yellow bell pepper
12 green olives (8 whole, 4 chopped)
1 tbsp cornstarch
1 tbsp salt to taste
Optional: 1 tsp adobo + 1 tsp salt
(instead of only salt)

For the meatballs:

28 oz frozen plant-based meatballs

Serves 8

Vegetable Stew

DIRECTIONS

1. Peel the carrots and potatoes. Cut into small cubes. Boil until tender. Don't soften too much because they will be cooked again later. Then remove them from the heat.

2. Cook meatballs according to the instructions in the package.

3. Base for the sauce: In 1/4 cup olive oil, sauté thinly chopped onion, garlic, and tomatoes until soft. Cook for about 10 minutes. Blend the mixture. Then add pepper, mustard, cumin, and bouillon cubes.

4. Rice preparation: In a skillet, sauté garlic, onion, and bell peppers in olive oil. Add rice and sauté for 5 minutes. Add water, bouillon cubes, and salt. Cook over low heat until rice is ready.

5. Final sauce: In another pan, heat 1/4 cup olive oil, fry bell peppers. When the peppers are soft, add the blended sauce base, olives, cornstarch, and salt (or salt and adobo to taste). Let the sauce reduce for about 5-10 minutes, or until the desired consistency is reached.

6. Combine and simmer: Add meatballs, potatoes, and carrots to the sauce. Let the meatballs and veggies cook in the sauce for 5-7 minutes, to allow flavors to develop.

Ready to savor a delightful vegetable stew!

Claudia and Silvia Quijada

"We got reunited in Los Angeles. Silvia came in 1999. On June 22, 2001, I arrived. We got there, and then we moved to Denver because we had another sister there, too. As time goes by, you get used to life here. [In El Salvador], one thinks that it is easy to live in the United States. One thinks that getting here is super easy. But here life is harder than there. Because here you work 24/7, you have no rest. It's your decision. If you want to progress, you are going to work harder.

In El Salvador, I worked at a European language academy. I was in charge of the academy. And when I got here, I went to clean rooms with [Silvia]. I cried. I cried because I couldn't clean the rooms, I couldn't clean them fast enough. [My sisters] helped me because they had more experience than me. I asked myself, 'Why did I come here?' I cried and cried. We started working at hotels. Then, later, we started cooking at home when I was pregnant. With Silvia, primarily.

It's nice to be able to share our food. Our food is very... homemade. So when Americans come to the restaurant, they tell us, "This food is delicious. It's like I cooked it." Salvadoran food is very elaborate. It is a lot of work. The process of making it is quite a bit of work. But it is delicious because it tastes homemade." (Claudia)

Black Bean Pupusas

INGREDIENTS

For the dough:

1 lb corn flour

2 cups water

2 tbsp vegetable oil

For the filling:

8 oz cooked black beans

8 oz grated queso fresco

4 tbsp cooking oil

STEPS

1. In a bowl, prepare the dough, mixing the flour, water, and oil.

2. In a frying pan, cook the black beans with 4 tbsp vegetable oil and garlic until they are cooked through and soft. Then, mash them until you get a uniform paste. Let the paste cool.

3. Take a portion of dough and form it into a ball. In your hand, roll out the dough to form a disk about 4-5 inches in diameter and 1/4 inch thick. Make an indentation in the center of the disc.

4. Fill the indentation with a tbsp of beans and a tbsp of grated cheese.

5. Close the dough over the filling, making sure to seal the edges well to prevent the filling from escaping. Use the "tap-tap" method, gently tapping with your hands to flatten and shape the pupusa.

6. Heat a griddle or frying pan over high heat. Next, cook the pupusa over medium-high heat for about 4-5 minutes on each side, or until golden brown and cooked through.

Enjoy your freshly made pupusas!

Loroco Pupusas

INGREDIENTS

For the dough:
1 lb corn flour
2 cups water
2 tbsp vegetable oil

For the filling:
1/2 lb of chopped loroco
(typical flower from El Salvador)
1/2 lb grated fresh cheese

STEPS

1. In a bowl, prepare the dough, mixing the flour, water, and oil.

2. In a large bowl, mix the chopped loroco (at room temperature) with the grated fresh cheese.

3. Take a portion of dough and form it into a ball. Make a well in the center of the dough ball.

4. Fill the hole with a generous portion of the loroco and fresh cheese mixture.

5. Seal the edges of the dough tightly around the filling, making sure they are tightly closed to prevent the filling from escaping.

6. Flatten the stuffed pupusa and cook on a hot griddle until golden brown on both sides, about 4-5 minutes per side.

We hope you enjoy these delicious loroco pupusas!

Spinach Pupusas

INGREDIENTS

For the dough:

1 lb corn flour

2 cups water

2 tbsp vegetable oil

For the filling:

1/4 chopped onion

1/4 chopped red bell pepper

1/4 chopped green bell pepper

1 lb chopped spinach

1/2 lb grated fresh cheese

STEPS

1. In a large bowl, prepare the dough by mixing the corn flour with water and oil. Add the water gradually and mix until you obtain a soft, pliable dough. Add the oil while kneading to make sure it is evenly distributed.

2. In a large skillet, sauté the onion, red bell pepper, and green bell pepper until tender. Then, add the chopped spinach and cook until it softens and releases its water. Remove from the heat and let cool. Add the cheese.

3. Take a portion of dough and form it into a ball. In your hand, roll out the dough to form a disk about 4-5 inches in diameter and 1/4 inch thick. Make a hole in the center of the disc.

4. Fill the hole with a generous tbsp of the vegetable and cheese mixture.

5. Close the dough over the filling, making sure to seal the edges well to prevent the filling from escaping. Use the "tap-tap" method, gently tapping with your hands to flatten and shape the pupusa.

6. Heat a griddle or skillet over medium-high heat and cook the pupusa for about 4-5 minutes on each side, or until golden and cooked through.

Now you can enjoy some delicious spinach and fresh cheese pupusas!

Zucchini Pupusas

INGREDIENTS

For the dough:

1 lb corn flour
2 cups water
2 tbsp vegetable oil

For the filling:

2 medium zucchini
1/2 lb grated fresh cheese

STEPS

1. In a large bowl, prepare the dough by mixing the corn flour with water and oil. Add water gradually and mix until you obtain a soft, pliable dough. Add the oil while kneading to make sure it is evenly distributed.

2. Grate the zucchini and place them in a colander. Sprinkle a little salt over the grated zucchini and squeeze the grated zucchini to remove excess liquid.

3. In a large bowl, mix the grated zucchini with the grated fresh cheese.

4. Take a portion of dough and form it into a ball. Make a well in the center of the dough ball.

5. Fill the hole with a generous portion of the zucchini and cheese mixture.

6. Seal the edges of the dough tightly around the filling, making sure they are tightly closed to prevent the filling from escaping.

7. Flatten the stuffed pupusa and cook on a hot griddle until golden brown on both sides, about 4-5 minutes per side.

I hope you enjoy these zucchini pupusas!

Shoeb Iqbal

"I came to the U.S. in November 2014, to Texas. Then, I was at the detention center for a week. After, they moved me to El Paso County Jail, in Colorado, and I was there for one month. That is like a prison, not an immigration center. After one month, they moved me to Colorado GEO Detention Center. I was there for 18 months. After 18 months, they moved me to Arizona. Arizona to Lousiana; Louisiana to Alabama. After that, I won my case again. Then they took me back again from Alabama to here [Colorado]. It's been a long journey, two and a half years in immigration detention centers."

"My mother passed when I was in the Alabama jail. After a week, I learned she'd passed. She had a brain stroke. I am planning to go back to Bangladesh in the future. [In the U.S.], you have everything, and you have nothing. No family. Loneliness is one of the most… I have everything, pretty much. I have a good job. I like what I'm doing, fighting for people. I have friends. I'm missing so much my family."

Update: In January 2024, after much hard work and struggle for 10 years, Shoeb became a U.S. citizen.

Bangladeshi Beef Stew

INGREDIENTS

For Marinating the Beef:

2 lbs boneless beef, bite-sized pieces

1/4 cup plain yogurt

2 tsp turmeric powder

2 tsp cumin powder

2 tsp coriander powder

Red chili powder to taste

Salt to taste

For the Stew:

4 tbsp vegetable oil

2 tsp cumin seeds

1 cinnamon stick

4-6 pods green cardamom

4-6 cloves

2 bay leaves

4 large yellow onions, finely sliced

4-6 cloves garlic, minced

2 inch piece of ginger, minced

4-6 green chiles, slit (to taste)

4 tomatoes, chopped

2 tsp turmeric powder

1 tsp ground coriander

2 tsp garam masala

Salt to taste

4 cups water (adjust for desired consistency)

4 ct carrots, peeled and sliced

4 ct potatoes, peeled and diced

Fresh cilantro leaves for garnish

Bangladeshi Beef Stew

DIRECTIONS

1. In a large mixing bowl, combine the beef pieces with yogurt, turmeric powder, cumin powder, coriander powder, red chili powder, and salt. Mix well to ensure the beef is coated evenly with the spices and yogurt. Allow the beef to marinate for a minimum of 30 minutes. Refrigerate it for a few hours for better flavor absorption.

2. Heat 4 tbsp vegetable oil in a large pot over medium heat. Add cumin seeds, cinnamon sticks, cardamom pods, cloves, and bay leaves. Sauté for 1 minute until aromatic. Add onions and sauté until golden brown.

3. Stir in the minced garlic, ginger, and green chilies. Sauté until fragrant.

4. Add the marinated beef to the pot. Cook over medium-high heat, stirring occasionally, until the beef is browned on all sides.

5. Add chopped tomatoes, turmeric powder, ground coriander, garam masala, and salt. Cook for 5-7 minutes until tomatoes break down.

6. Pour in water, mix well. Bring to a boil, then simmer covered for 1.5-2 hours until beef is tender and stew thickens.

7. Add the sliced carrots and diced potatoes to the stew. Continue simmering for an additional 20-30 minutes or until the carrots and potatoes are tender.

8. Adjust the seasoning with salt and garam masala to taste. Garnish the Bangladeshi beef stew with fresh cilantro leaves.

9. Serve hot with steamed rice or flatbreads like naan or paratha.

Renato Fierro

"There are lots of people who have credit. I have never had credit. That's an American thing, I think. It is not an undocumented person thing. I have never bought a car from a dealership either, making payments, signing a contract, that type of stuff. I've never done it. I always think that's an American thing. A citizen thing. Any citizen of their country can sign a contract. That's a citizen thing, getting a contract easily, getting a loan. You have more open doors to get a loan. Because you have more open doors to find a job, a good job, a stable job. There are always ways in which they close the doors to you even if you have some protection. And the bad thing is you can lose it any minute. I don't make plans. I don't have stability. If I wanted to buy a car, it's not just because of the credit but also because of that. My permit is for 2 years. What happens after the 2 years? I can't guarantee that I'll be here. Then I'll lose the car, right, will lose the contract and all of that. And it's the same with houses. I don't know why buy a house if I don't know what will happen. I get deported, and what will happen to the house? This is only every 2 years, every 2 years. That's the time I plan."

"My father was deported. He was here like 26 years, paying his taxes and all, working in construction. He has never asked for any government help or anything. He's never even gone to the hospital, even if he felt bad. He worked in construction. He stepped on a nail once, one of the big ones they use for framing, but he didn't go to the hospital or anything. It happened to his hand too. He cut his hand. He's never been to the hospital, as far as I know. But they didn't care. When I went to speak with the immigration officer, I told him, "Look, he's paying his taxes…" And I showed him documents and all. They didn't care about any of that."

Renato Fierro

You become more aware of your immigration status in high school. I already knew since middle school but didn't understand it very well. I switched to high school, and that's when I started to realize that many different opportunities were closing doors on me. If I go to college and get a degree, what for? If I can be deported. I make a big mistake, like driving under the influence of alcohol or whatever, and I can be deported. I know people who have charges for driving under the influence and those kinds of things and nothing happens to them, but I'm always a little more paranoid. So I didn't want to... Sometimes I do feel like going back, but that's always on my mind. My immigration status is what holds me back from going to other states, from traveling. That's what always holds me back. That's what I notice with many other people too. But there are also other people who are undocumented and don't care. They go everywhere, they travel. But that's how I lived, in fear, afraid of who's on the other side of the door. That's why I don't dare to do so many things, because of the fear of the consequences.

Sometimes I've talked to other people who have DACA. You know they're trying to eliminate it. In 2017, when they tried to do it... after Trump said 'I have heart', 'I'm going to show my heart to those who have DACA', Jeff Sessions said 'We're going to end DACA'. Oh, what a big heart Trump has! It changes your emotions, your self-esteem. Sometimes you're very optimistic and other times you become very pessimistic. Sometimes I'm quite pessimistic. But then, the truth is that they did renew my DACA, which gives me a little more optimism. Things change all the time.

Espaguetis con Estofado Casero

Serves 6

INGREDIENTS

6 ct Roma tomatoes

1 jalapeño

1 medium yellow onion

2 tbsp crushed garlic

1 1/2 tsp Adobo

6 cups water

Salt & pepper to taste

2 tbsp vegetable oil

1 packet ground sausage

2 boxes dry spaghetti

DIRECTIONS

1. Make the sauce by boiling medium-cut tomatoes and minced jalapeño in a saucepan. Reduce heat after bringing to a boil and simmer for 5 minutes. Drain, reserving 1 cup of liquid.

2. While the sauce simmers, sauté chopped onion until translucid. Add garlic and continue to sauté for another 3 minutes, stirring periodically.

3. Blend tomatoes, jalapeño, onion, and garlic with 1 cup of the liquid used to boil the tomatoes and the Adobo until well-blended. Leave some texture.

4. Boil water for pasta, adding 1 tbsp of salt.

5. In a medium pan, heat 1 tbsp oil and brown sausage on medium-high heat. Season with salt and pepper to taste.

6. Combine the tomato sauce from the blender with the browned sausage in the pan. Reduce on medium heat for 5 minutes.

7. Boil pasta in salted water. Drain in a colander when softened.

8. Immediately mix the sauce with the pasta and serve.

Consider using vegetarian sausage for a meatless-pasta alternative.

Senait Ketema

"My hopes were to get my education and my husband's education and to go back to Ethiopia. That was my hope.

I never went back. Due to political situations in Ethiopia, most of my husband's friends were killed. And our families told us not to come back, so we asked for asylum and stayed here.

It was difficult. Very difficult. It was. I still have the suitcases I bought to take my stuff with me to Ethiopia. I show my kids those suitcases. They are downstairs in the basement. Yeah, that's the most difficult thing. Not to have your family around. When you are so close to your family, and, all of a sudden, that was not your wish, but it happened."

"No one wants to leave their country *just because* and go to a strange place where they know no one, where they have to start from scratch. There is a reason. Whether the reason is good enough to the other person or not, there is a reason why one cannot or is not able to stay in their country. So I wish (people in the host country) found out, that we could help them understand that all immigrants are not criminals, that it's not that immigrants don't know anything. That's not true. Actually, a lot of immigrants are intelligent; they are hard workers. The reason they came here is not to be a burden on somebody. They came here to make a life for them, and for their children, and for the families they left at home."

Miser Wat

Spicy Red Lentil Stew

INGREDIENTS

1 cup red lentils
4-5 ct garlic cloves
1-2 tbsp canola oil
1 yellow onion, minced
2 tsp-1 tbsp berbere
3-4 cup water
Salt to taste

DIRECTIONS

1. Rinse and drain the lentils.

2. Peel and mince the garlic.

3. Heat the oil in a saucepan, sauté the onion until translucent.

4. Add berbere, stir until well coated. Add garlic and cook until flavors meld (about 5 minutes).

5. Add water to blend, then stir in lentils until well coated. Add ½ teaspoon salt and 3 cups of water.

6. Cook until lentils break apart, adjusting water if needed. Aim for a thick stew consistency.

7. Taste and adjust salt. Your flavorful Miser Wat is ready to be savored!

Yekik Alicha

INGREDIENTS

1 1/2 yellow onion
1-1 1/2 tbsp garlic cloves
1-1 1/2 fresh ginger
1 cup yellow split peas
1/4 cup cooking oil
1/2 tsp turmeric
3 cups water
Salt to taste
Optional garnish: sliced
jalapeños, chopped red bell
pepper

Mild Yellow Split Pea Stew

DIRECTIONS

1. Mince the onions. Peel and puree the garlic cloves and the ginger.

2. Boil split peas, drain, and set aside.

3. Sauté onions in oil until golden. Add garlic, ginger, turmeric, and split peas.

4. Add 3 cups of water, bring to boil, then simmer until peas are soft and stew is thick (about 30 minutes).

5. Season with salt and garnish if desired.

Enjoy your vibrant Yekik Alicha!

Tikil Gomen

Cabbage and Carrot Stew

INGREDIENTS

1 1/2 medium yellow onions

3 large carrots

2 potatoes

1 jalepeño

1 tbsp puréed fresh garlic

1 tsp puréed fresh peeled ginger

8-10 cup green cabbage

1/2 cup canola oil

1/4 tsp tumeric

1/4 tsp salt

1/4 tsp black pepper

1 cup water

DIRECTIONS

1. Thinly slice the onions. Slice the carrots diagonally. Peel and cut the potatoes in small-medium cubes. Chop jalapeño (you can remove seeds for a less spicy dish or leave them). Peel and mash the ginger and garlic. Chop the cabbage.

2. Sauté the onions in oil until golden. Add the carrots, then the potatoes. Cover and cook until the potatoes are slightly tender.

3. Add garlic, ginger, turmeric, salt, and pepper. Cook for an additional minute.

4. Pour in water, stir, and add cabbage and jalapeño. Cook until vegetables are soft.

5. Serve immediately and savor the delicious Tikil Gomen!

Authentic Injera
(Ethiopian Flatbread)

La Blanca, Guatemala

Guadalupe (Lupe) Lopez

"I have Guatemalan blood, but I was born in Chiapas. My husband is from Oaxaca, México. In the year 2000, we got married and we have 5 children who are U.S. citizens. Two boys are in high school, two girls are in middle school, and we have a 3-year-old baby. We are a loving family. Sadly, in 2012, we were pulled over by the state police because my husband was going 8 miles over the speed limit. The officer approached the car and told my husband, 'I pulled you over because you were going 8 miles past the speed limit. Give me your license, insurance, and car registration. I'll give you a ticket and you can go.' But when he saw my husband gave him a Mexican license, he went to his vehicle and made a call on the radio. He came back and said, 'Step out of the car. I need you to sign your ticket and you can go.' But it wasn't that way. He arrested my husband while other officers arrived. They asked us for documents and asked questions, 'How come you speak English? Where are you from? Are you here legally?' We didn't know our rights. We answered everything. The officer said, 'We work as immigration officers.' Then we learned about 287(g).* It is because of 287(g) that we are in deportation proceedings. We don't know what will happen in our future. My son is 17 and will graduate high school in a year. We worry because our last court appointment is in January 2020 and his graduation is in May 2020. We don't know if we'll be able to be there to see him graduate. My children dream of finishing college. They have the right to live without fear. This is their country and they shouldn't have to live in fear."

*Through Section 287(g) of the U.S. Immigration and Nationality Act, ICE provides select state and local enforcement officers with authorization to identify, process, and sometimes even detain immigration offenders they encounter during their regular, daily law-enforcement activity.

Potato & Cheese Empanadas

Serves 4

INGREDIENTS

For the Crust:

3 cups Maseca instant yellow corn
    masa flour

2 tbsp of salt

2 ¼ cups warm water

For the Filling:

2 large russet potatoes

1 medium yellow onion, chopped small

1 tsp fresh garlic, minced

¼ cup sour cream

1 cup shredded cheese
   (we used cheddar)

¼ tsp cayenne pepper

1 tsp parsley, chopped

Salt and pepper to taste

For garnish:

2 tomatoes

1 jalapeño

1 cup water

Salt and pepper to taste

2 cups of shredded white cabbage

1 cup crumbled 'queso fresco'

For cooking:

1 3/4 cups of vegetable oil for frying

2 pieces of round plastic cut out from
   a bag (freezer bags work great)

Potato & Cheese Empanadas

DIRECTIONS

1. Prepare the dough: mix the Maseca flour, salt, and warm water in a bowl, to form a ball. Knead until smooth.

2. Bring the oven to 400°F. Rinse the tomatoes and remove the stems. Roast the tomatoes for about 20 minutes. This will lower the acidity and sweeten them. Put the tomatoes in the blender, along with the jalapeños and 1 cup of water. Add salt and pepper to taste.

3. Turn the oven down to 350°F. Bake the potatoes until tender and fully cooked. Let the potato cool slightly and peel. Place it in a medium bowl and mash it.

4. Preheat 1/4 cup of oil at medium-high temperature. Add the onion and sauté until translucid. Add the garlic and sauté 2 minutes. Let cool for 5 minutes.

5. Combine the potatoes, onion, garlic, and the rest of the ingredients for the filling.

6. Divide the dough into 10 balls. Place one ball between two pieces of round plastic and press using a tortilla press (a heavy skillet or a dish work for this, too).

7. Remove the top piece of plastic and spoon some stuffing onto the tortilla. Leave room to seal the edges.

8. Supporting your hand with the bottom plastic, fold the dough to make a half moon-shaped turnover. Pinch the edges. You can use a fork to seal, too. Here, we make sure that the empanada won't leak when fried.

9. Remove the empanada from the plastic. Set aside on a large plate. Repeat with the rest of the dough and filling.

10. Heat 1 1/2 cup oil in a skillet over high heat. Time to fry!

11. Deep fry the empanadas one or two at a time until golden brown (~2 minutes on each side). Drain them on a plate covered with paper towels. Serve them topped with the sauce, queso fresco, and cabbage.

Carlos Blanco

"They wanted to rob you for anything, so... and there was a time—at the time when I came here—I'm talking about 2007, 2008, when they forced all those young people to join the gangs. It wasn't… they didn't ask, 'Do you want to join?' They forced people. You had to get in and that's it. I mean, imagine: What if I had stayed? What would have come of that? Some classmates from school went through that. More than anything, women say that, that they were forced, that is... 'I like you and you're going to be my woman,' and all that. I mean, it's ugly. And other colleagues told me, 'They made me drive. They told me: *You're going to drive, come on, come on. Learn to drive, to drive cars.*' And that's it. In other words, they didn't ask if they wanted to. They had to do it, otherwise, they would be

killed. This is what—well yes, this is what God freed me from because if not, imagine what would have happened to me. Could I have survived? I don't know how I'd be... without a leg, or without a hand, or with some bullets in my body, or all tattooed. Or the houses. Lots of people went to the colonies and said, 'Hey, I like this house.' The would get into the colonies and rang people's doorbells, 'We like your house. Leave. If you don't get out today, we are going to kill you.' So, imagine. Wow, ma'am, I don't know... These are houses that people worked for for years, that have cost them so much. This was the inheritance for the children. And these gangs come and take them away just like that. Many people left houses, left cars, left everything because of that. Because, since they took over everything, people in fear preferred to leave their stuff and just go; it's- it's life. I mean, all of that. And I freed myself from all of that. If not, imagine how I'd be. And now I tell you, if they ask me if I go to my country... Yes, I do but for tourism, I mean, what can I ... what future can I expect for my children there?"

Carlos Blanco

"In 2010, a law was passed here that anyone who didn't have a Colorado driver's license couldn't drive. So, it happened to me. I was stopped for something that- just for- like routine, for a routine stop. So, they stopped me, asked for my license. At that time, I didn't have a license and, well, there it began. Then, the social security, well, didn't have that either. If you don't have a license, how are you going to have a social security number? I mean... In 2010 they stopped me and since 2010 they've been fighting my case in immigration, so... Like I said, many people... When I fell into the detention center there were many people: 'Why were you stopped? Why did they stop you?' 'Well, because I didn't have a light on, I didn't stay in a lane, because I didn't use the turn signal, I turned right, I turned left, I was like that, they thought I was drunk.' Well, for something insignificant. That law was SB-70, I think, something like that. So, that... anyone who didn't have... straight to immigration. Well, I fell into that. So, since then I've been in this mess. I mean. I don't know why the system, well, in this country works like that, right? For something... just because, right? Because I tell you, there are people who, well, deserve to be here and there are people who don't deserve to be here, I mean, right? Because there are people who just come to this country to create trouble; they come to take advantage of the country's situation, of the aid and everything, right? Or they do their thing and they take housing, they take stuff and destroy them, or they do, well, pure bad things. I don't, well, here I am up to date with my taxes, paying rent, paying here, paying everything, working well. So I don't know why, right - why they don't look at that, why they don't do the famous immigration reform they talk about. Every time there are elections, lately, immigrants are the talking point."

Chicken Sandwich

INGREDIENTS

3 chicken breasts

1 bag Relajo spice mix

4 Roma tomatoes

3 tbsp achiote powder

1 cucumber

8oz radish

6 bolillos (bread)

Mayonnaise to taste

Mustard to taste

Watercress, for garnish

DIRECTIONS

1. Heat the oven to 400°F. Place the chicken in a large pot and cover it with water. Cook it in the oven for about 30 minutes or until the chicken is tender and fully cooked. Remove the chicken, reserving 2 cups of the broth for the sauce.

2. In a blender, combine the spice packet, 2 chopped tomatoes, the 2 cups of reserved chicken broth, and achiote powder. Blend until smooth.

3. Place the chicken in the same pot used for boiling (no water this time) and cover it evenly with the sauce you prepared. Bake the chicken in the preheated oven for about 20 minutes. The sauce should thicken slightly, and the flavors should become more concentrated.

4. Once the chicken is cool enough to handle, shred it or cut it into thin slices.

5. Slice the 2 tomatoes that you have left, the cucumber, and the radish thinly.

6. Cut the Bolillo rolls in half along the top. Spread mayonnaise and mustard on the sides. On the sides of each roll, align slices of cucumber, tomato, and radish vertically. Add a generous portion of the baked chicken in the center. Garnish with fresh watercress.

Franyerson Puerta

"I came from Venezuela for two reasons. I was a soldier in Venezuela, and I didn't agree with politics and all that. So I deserted. The government was looking for me. I put my son, my wife, and my mother at risk. Another reason I came to the United States was because of my boxing career. To be able to fulfill my dream of being world champion here in the United States. First I went to Colombia. I asked for political asylum in Colombia, but the country did not provide me with any support from political security. And that's why I had to migrate here, to the United States. I came to the United States with my wife, my son, my sister, my brother-in-law, and my nephew. We came by land. We had to go through the jungle of Colombia, the jungle of Panama... It took us 12 days to get to Mexico. We crossed the Darien jungle. In the jungle we lasted two and a half days. To be able to get out of the jungle, the jungle is very complicated. Very dangerous. Not a route for us really. But well, we all look for that route to get to the United States because there is no other. Along the way, we went through a lot of work, especially with the children. Inside the jungle, too, there is a lot of danger. Both with mafias, with animals... It's a jungle. After we arrived in Bajo Chiquito, in Panama, the situation was different. The danger was not the jungle. Every country we entered, we were not welcome. They take your money. They rape women, abuse children. A lot of xenophobia."

8 servings

Mushroom Sauce

INGREDIENTS

1 pound mushrooms

2 tbsp olive oil

A pinch of garlic salt

4 1/4 cups milk

4 1/4 cups whipping cream

A pinch of oregano

A pinch of sugar

DIRECTIONS

1. Clean and slice mushrooms.

2. Heat 2 tbsp of olive oil in a pot over medium heat. Add the sliced mushrooms and garlic salt to the skillet. Sauté until the mushrooms are tender, about 5-7 minutes.

3. Add milk to the pot. Allow it to boil.

4. Once the milk is boiling, add the whipping cream. Stir in the pinch of oregano. Mix well until the ingredients are fully incorporated.

5. Allow the sauce to simmer gently over low heat for about 10-15 minutes, stirring occasionally, until it thickens slightly and the flavors meld together.

6. Taste the sauce and adjust the seasoning if needed. Add a pinch of sugar. Add more salt or oregano, according to your preference.

7. Serve the creamy mushroom sauce hot over your favorite pasta, grilled chicken, steak, or any dish of your choice.

Cordon Bleu

INGREDIENTS

Aluminum foil
2 chicken breasts
4 slices Swiss cheese
4 slices prosciutto
2 tbsp cooking oil

DIRECTIONS

1. Lay out a sheet of aluminum foil large enough to wrap each chicken breast individually. Place a chicken breast on each piece of foil.

2. Layer 2 slices of Swiss cheese and 2 slices of prosciutto on top of each chicken breast. Roll up the chicken breasts, enclosing the cheese and prosciutto inside. Wrap each rolled chicken breast tightly in aluminum foil, ensuring they are fully sealed.

3. Bring a large pot of water to a boil over high heat. Once boiling, carefully add the foil-wrapped chicken breasts to the pot. Reduce the heat to medium-low, and let the chicken breasts simmer in the boiling water for 20-25 minutes, or until cooked through. Once cooked, remove the foil-wrapped chicken breasts from the pot and carefully unwrap them. To ensure the chicken is cooked through, use a meat thermometer to check for an internal temperature of 165°F, or by ensuring the meat is opaque with clear juices running out when cut into.

4. Heat a skillet over medium-high heat, add 2 tbsp oil, and sauté the chicken breasts for 2-3 minutes on each side, or until golden brown and crispy. Remove from the skillet, and let them rest for a few minutes before serving.

Enjoy your homemade Chicken Cordon Bleu!

Salsa Verde

INGREDIENTS

6 eggs
1 cup cooking oil
4 sprigs of cilantro
1 head of garlic
A pinch of salt
A pinch of sugar

DIRECTIONS

1. Add the 6 raw eggs to the blender. Blend for 20 seconds.

2. With the blender still on, add the oil very slowly. Keep the blender running for about 45 seconds.

3. Rinse the cilantro sprigs under cold water to remove any dirt or debris. Place the cilantro leaves and stems in the blender. Peel the garlic cloves, and add them to the blender or food processor. Add a pinch of salt and a pinch of sugar to the blender. Blend the ingredients until you get a smooth (mayo-textured) paste.

Sabe Kemer

"[My mom taught me] that cooking is a way to connect with people. Cooking is a way to show your love for your family and your community. Cooking is a time to share your day, to share what's going on in your life. It's therapeutic. Food is healing. And being around other people, being around the people you love, and sharing a meal is therapeutic. In many ways. Spiritually, physically, communally... [In my culture] Typically, cooking is done by moms or older sisters. Eating time, whether you know how to cook or not, everybody's there. Typically, family members of 10–15, and, if you add neighbors, typical dinner can turn into a party of 20 before you know it. It's a communal thing.

What I miss the most about Ethiopia is the fact that everyone knows everyone. I am from a small village. If I went from our village to the next village, people knew who I was. Young people, elderly people, everyone knows each other. That sense of oneness, unity. I miss that. In Ethiopia, your neighbors invite you for coffee very frequently or you invite your neighbors for coffee. Even though I was a child at the time, I still remember the laughter and the people that often gathered over coffee and over meals and such. I miss that a lot, actually."

Serves 4

Ethiopian Beef Tips

INGREDIENTS

1.5 lb beef sirloin

1 tsp salt

1 lemon

1 tsp black pepper

4 medium cloves of garlic

2 tbsp ginger

1 medium onion

1 tbsp vegetable oil

2 tbsp berbere

5 tbsp spiced butter-unsalted

1 tsp cumin

A pinch of rosemary-dried

Optional: 1 jalapeño pepper

DIRECTIONS

1. Cut the beef into bite-sized pieces. Season them lightly with salt.

2. Heat a large skillet over medium-high heat. Without adding oil initially, add the beef cubes to the skillet. Squeeze the juice from half a lemon over the beef and sprinkle with black pepper. Sear the beef without stirring for 1-2 minutes until a golden crust forms, then stir to cook until most of the water evaporates.

3. Mince the garlic and ginger. Chop 1/2 onion and slice 1/2 onion.

4. When the meat softens and the water from the meat evaporates, add the oil, 1/2 chopped onion, 1/2 sliced onion, minced garlic, and ginger. Continue cooking until the meat is nearly done.

5. Add the berbere spice mix, spiced butter, cumin, and rosemary to the skillet. Stir well to coat the beef thoroughly with the spices. Cook for 2-3 minutes to allow the flavors to meld. If the mixture seems dry, add a little more spiced butter or a splash of water to keep it moist.

6. If using, add the sliced jalapeño and cook for another minute. Adjust the seasoning with more salt, pepper, or berbere according to your taste.

Ethiopian Veggie Tips

INGREDIENTS

1 tsp vegetable oil

1 1/2 medium onions

1 tsp black pepper

1 tsp rosemary-dried

2 bags plant-based seared tips

2 tbsp ginger

4 medium cloves of garlic

1 lemon

5 tbsp spiced butter-unsalted

2 tbsp berbere

1 tsp salt

1 tsp cumin

Optional: 1 jalapeño pepper

DIRECTIONS

1. Heat a large skillet with 1 tsp oil over medium-high heat. Chop 1 onion and sauté it with 1 tsp black pepper and a pinch of dried rosemary until softened.

2. Add the meatless meat (tips) to the skillet. Stir in 2 tbsp of minced ginger, garlic, and the juice from 1/2 lemon. Cook until the tips soften, adding water to prevent sticking.

3. Slice 1/2 onion. Once the tips have softened, add the onion and 1 tbsp of spiced butter to the skillet. Continue to simmer until the flavors blend.

4. Add the berbere spice mix, 4 tbsp of spiced butter, salt, cumin, and a pinch of dried rosemary to the skillet. Stir well to coat the beef thoroughly with the spices. Cook for 2-3 minutes to allow the flavors to meld. If the mixture seems dry, add a little more spiced butter or a splash of water to keep it moist.

5. If desired, add the sliced jalapeño to the skillet and cook for another minute. Adjust the seasoning with more salt, pepper, or berbere according to your taste.

Jesus y Alberli Marte

"I decided to leave Venezuela because I had a problem. They burned down my house there. They wanted me to pay *vacuna**, but I refused. I went out around 3 in the afternoon to find something to eat. And when I got back there, they had already burned down the house. I had to flee. I went to another municipality. There, I waited for a week and then went to Ecuador. I emigrated. I spent two years in Ecuador with my wife. My wife was pregnant. We spent two years there. My wife gave birth there. And then we decided to go to the United States to give a better life to my family, to the children we left there in Venezuela."

"The mafia wanted me to work for them. I didn't want to work for them. They were asking for 'vacuna', but I refused. They told me to sell drugs, but I didn't want to. They gave me 48 hours to leave the house, but I didn't leave. I thought they were bluffing. They waited for me to leave, and then they burned down the house around 4:30 in the afternoon. My wife was at her mom's when that happened. She called me. She stayed at her mom's for two days. I left, and she followed me. We went to Colombia. From Colombia, we went straight to Ecuador." (Jesus)

*vacuna= extortion by a criminal organization for not working for the organization

Serves 10

Sancocho

INGREDIENTS

3 lbs ribs

2 corn cobs

2 plantains

2 medium carrots

6 potatoes

4 tsp chicken bouillon powder

1 acorn squash

1/2 tbsp salt

1 tsp black pepper

1 tbsp vegetable oil

DIRECTIONS

1. Cut the meat into bites. Season with salt and black pepper. You can also use adobo, garlic powder, or onion powder, to taste. Marinate for about 30 minutes.

2. Peel the yuca, potatoes, carrots, and plantains, and cut them into 1-inch pieces. Husk the corn and slice it into 2-inch-thick segments. As you peel and cut, place the veggies in separate containers with enough water to cover them.

3. In a large pot, heat 1 tablespoon oil over medium-high. When the oil is hot, add the meat and brown it on all sides for 5 minutes.

4. Add 6-8 cups of water and 4 tsp bouillon powder. Simmer the meat until partially cooked and tender, for about 45 minutes.

5. To keep the vegetables from falling apart, you will add them to the pot with the meat in order of firmness. When the meat has been boiling for about 45 minutes, add the yuca and plantains. Add more liquid as needed. Cook on medium-high for another 30 minutes. Then add the carrots and potatoes. Add more liquid, as needed, and simmer on low for another 45 minutes to 1 hour.

7. Simmer all vegetables and the meat until they are all tender. Check the seasoning and add more, as needed.

Erika Vargas Reyes

"When I arrived in Wisconsin, I started to work. I found—thank God—I found two jobs: in a buffet and the other job was making snow cakes in a factory. When I arrived they paid me six dollars an hour, which was too little. [Laughs] But that was enough to send to my parents. The problem was that I arrived here and I didn't have any family here. Nobody. My whole family was in Mexico. And when we got here, the situation became too difficult and critical. Since I didn't have enough money for rent or food, I got together with a person live together, as a couple. That person was a very good person, but I got pregnant after six months. At that time, I weighed 95 pounds, I had two jobs and I had a threat of miscarriage because my body was not withstanding having two jobs, not eating well, and being pregnant. I went to the emergency room, there in Madison, and they told me that they couldn't do anything, that the solution was in my hands: if I wanted to have the baby, I would stop working; or, if I didn't want to have the baby, I ould continue working, and I was just going to have a miscarriage. If I wanted to have the baby, I had to stop working. So it was a very difficult situation but I chose to have my baby... who, by the way, was a girl, and that girl is now 19 years old and is in college studying in Auraria. On December 14, 2004, my baby was born. It was a very difficult stage of my life. My baby was due at the end of January and was born on December 14th. I went into a lot of depression. We were close to Christmas. I was very angry with my baby. It was a very difficult situation that I now tell my daughter about. I tell her: "It's not that I didn't love you at that time. It was just the hormones, the depression, I was alone. I needed my mom. I needed a lot of help and I didn't get it."

Squash Dessert

INGREDIENTS

2 butternut squash

1 cinnamon stick

1 bag of peanuts (0.5-0.75 lbs)

4 piloncillos (raw sugar cones)

DIRECTIONS

1. Peel the squash, and remove the seeds. Cut them into small cubes. Save the seeds.

2. In a large pot, combine the cubed squash and cinnamon stick with enough water to cover them. Bring to a boil, then reduce the heat and simmer until the squash is tender, about 15-20 minutes.

3. While the squash is cooking, crush the piloncillos into smaller pieces.

4. Once the squash is tender, drain it and return it to the pot.

5. Add the crushed piloncillos to the pot with the squash. Also, add the bag of peanuts.

6. Cook the mixture over medium heat, stirring occasionally, until the piloncillos are completely melted and the mixture thickens, about 15-20 minutes.

7. Remove the pot from the heat and let the *dulce de calabaza* (squash dessert) cool slightly before serving.

Maracay, Venezuela
Yosber Alexis

"The hardest part is leaving your family. It's the worst part. When you set off and have to say goodbye to your mother, or your brother, or the most beloved person you have by your side at that moment. And you leave with the uncertainty of what will happen along the way. The worst is when you separate yourself from your family. You don't know when you'll see them again or if you'll ever see them again. Regardless of whether it's with papers or without papers, it hurts. We are all human beings. We all have families. We all hope to reunite with them again. And you don't know what awaits you. Many say they will return to their country. But that is totally false because you don't know what life has prepared for you. Whether it's in that country or somewhere else. So, saying goodbye is the worst because you don't know if you will see them again. It's like uncertainty. You don't know what will happen. You don't know if a family member will die or if you will have the opportunity to see them again. You just don't know."

"The worst part of this journey was having to deal with so much evil along the way. Humanity is very corrupt. You realize that even though you are a good person, you encounter a lot of evil on the path that you have to face."

Yosber Alexis

"I decided to leave Venezuela because there was persecution. Politically against my family, since we had benefited from the government for a long time through public institutions. Strangers would come to our house; we had an obligation under the socialist policy of Venezuela to vote for mayors, governors, or even the president of Venezuela, since  we had benefited from public education and public health institutions. They would threaten my parents, and me too, as I was of age, that if we did not vote as they said, our lives would be in danger.

When I left Venezuela, I left most of my family behind since they all are still in Venezuela. Both my father and mother stayed in Venezuela. They did not have the same opportunity we did to flee from Venezuelan politics. If we had not fled, our parents would still be in great danger. That was the best decision, as we were heavily oppressed by the laws imposed by the government and we had no future to progress. So we made the decision to... it was either remain in that government slavery with those policies that did not benefit us at all, that gave us no advantage to study, to have a better future, or it was to try to flee from the politics and migrate to another country like the United States."

Serves 10

Venezuelan Quesillo

INGREDIENTS

For the quesillo:

10 eggs

1 3/4 cups powdered milk

1 can condensed milk

3/4 cup sugar

2 1/2 cups liquid milk

1 tbsp vanilla essence

For the caramel:

3/4 cup sugar

DIRECTIONS

Preparing the Caramel:
1. In a flan mold, place the 3/4 cup of sugar and let it melt until it turns golden brown. Continue stirring over heat until the sugar is completely dissolved, without any sugar grains or lumps. Remove from the heat. Let it cool and solidify.

Preparing the Quesillo:
1. Preheat the oven to 340°F.

2. In a large bowl, add the 10 eggs, and beat them well. Incorporate the powdered milk, and mix until smooth. Add the condensed milk, and continue mixing. Incorporate the sugar, liquid milk, and vanilla. Mix until you get a smooth mixture.

3. Pour the mixture into the caramel-coated mold, making sure to distribute it evenly. Cover the mold with aluminum foil.

4. Place the mold in a larger tray and fill it with hot water, creating a water bath. Bake in a water bath at 340°F for approximately 1 1/2 hour. To check for doneness, insert a toothpick into the center; if it comes out clean, the quesillo is ready.

5. Remove from the oven, and let it cool to room temperature. Refrigerate for at least 4 hours or preferably overnight. Unmold the quesillo and serve.

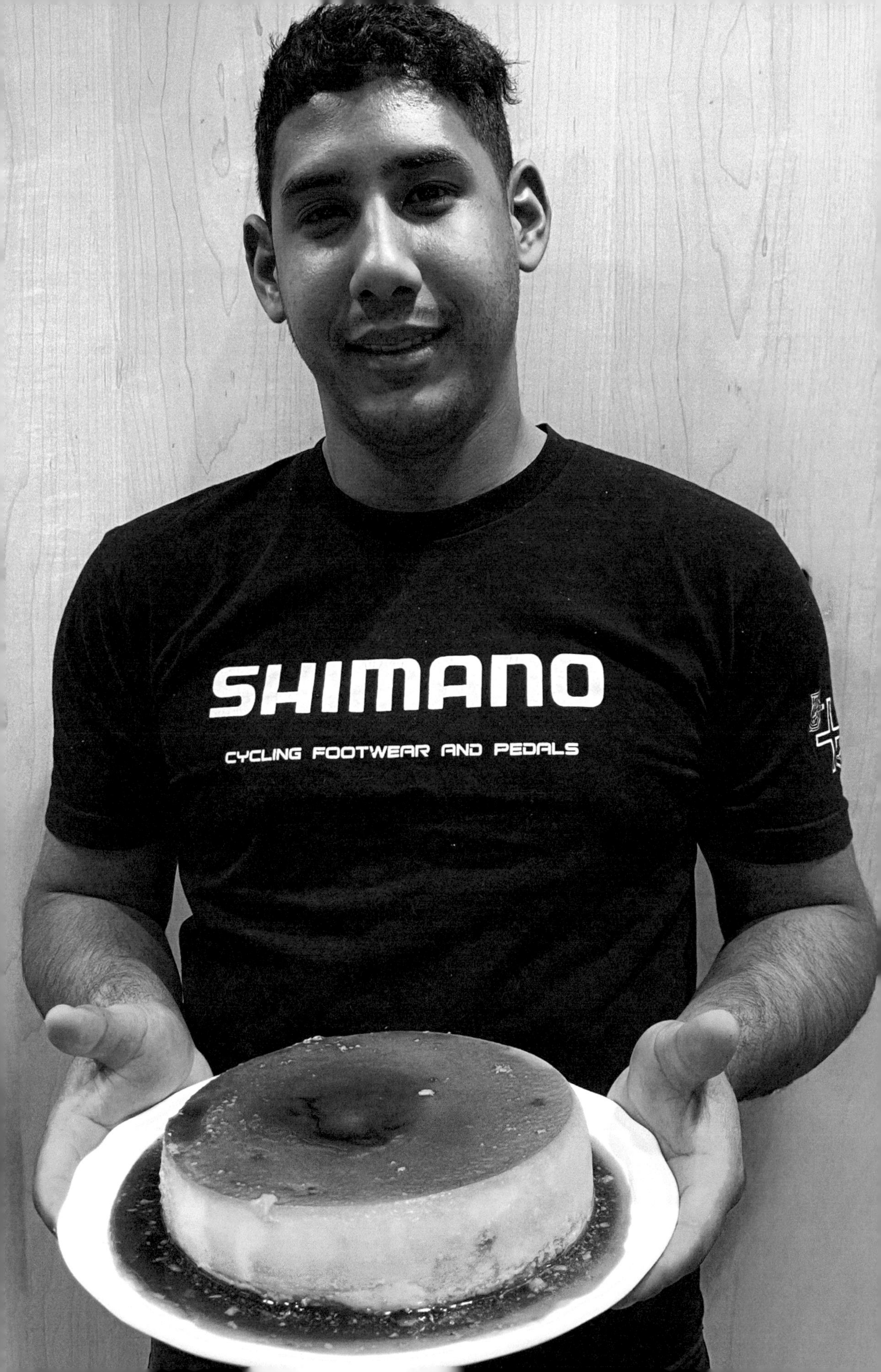
SHIMANO
CYCLING FOOTWEAR AND PEDALS

Gabriela Medina

"We had a bad experience when my husband faced the immigration system. It all started in 2012, in December. He previously worked in a bar, as security. And he met the people there. Later, he left the bar because everything was very tiring, working at night, and went to work in construction. And one day when he was coming back, well, one of those times when you feel like having a beer and you don't think of what's going to happen... He decided to go to the bar where he previously worked. We had a standard car. And it was snowing that day. And he was at the place, it was fine, he had a couple of beers, but it wasn't at a level of alcohol where he couldn't drive. Then when he left the place, the car, because it was standard, broke down. He went zigzagging. A police officer looked at him and stopped him. Then my husband stopped and tried to explain what had happened but the police officer didn't understand him. He went to the patrol car and came back and asked him questions. And my husband said, "I don't understand you, I don't understand you." And then he just said, "Get out of the car." "He got out and the police handcuffed him and took him away."

"He fell into the immigration system. They told him he had to pay $12,000 if he wanted to leave. Once again it was a pilgrimage. To gather again, to borrow, to raise the money so that he could get out. It was all in December. It was all in December. My children's birthday is in December, my son on the 7th and my daughter on the 22nd. And this was their first days of December, the 4th and 5th. They were little and didn't know what was happening. I told them, "Your dad went to work." What could I tell them!? During the day I took them to school, I was fine. But at night, I didn't sleep, I cried, I thought "What am I going to do?" Thank God, they didn't leave my hand. People who I didn't mention what was happening and who found out, came home. They supported us in ways that... I am so grateful because I felt alone because I didn't have my family here. But I had friends who had become my family. They were the ones who helped us get out at that time. They came with food, with things that I didn't ask for. I thank you with my heart. They say that gratitude is the memory of the heart, and I have so much gratitude. Every time I can do something for someone else, I do it."

Impossible Dessert

INGREDIENTS

1 can of condensed milk

1 can of evaporated milk

8 eggs

1 tbsp of vanilla essence

4 oz (half a stick) cream cheese

1 box of chocolate cake

Vegetable oil and eggs,
as instructed on the cake box

Dulce de leche topping,
squeeze bottle

STEPS

1. Preheat the oven to 350°F.

2. In a blender, mix the condensed milk, evaporated milk, eggs, cream cheese, and vanilla essence until well combined. This mixture is for the flan.

3. In another bowl, prepare the chocolate cake mix following the cake box directions.

4. In a flan bowl, squeeze dulce de leche topping. Then pour in the chocolate cake mix. Finally, on one side, slowly pour the flan mixture. Cover the mold with aluminum foil.

5. Place the mold inside a larger baking sheet, and add hot water to the baking sheet, creating a double boiler.

6. Bake in the preheated oven for about 1 hour and 30 minutes, or until a toothpick inserted into the center comes out clean.

7. Remove from the oven, and let cool to room temperature. Once cool, refrigerate for at least 4 hours or overnight.

Julia & Delio

When we were invited by Sarah (Jackson) to write a cookbook, we had never done anything remotely like it. We had never written a book; we didn't know how to use a camera well; and we certainly were not great cooks! We had our reservations but trusted that our experience working with immigrants would carry us forward. In our personal and professional lives, we had heard enough immigrant stories that <u>had</u> to be shared. We firmly believed (and still do) that listening to understand is a superpower—one that has the potential to address many modern-day challenges. So, we plunged head on…

See, there's something very intimate that occurs while cooking and eating… a bond that extends past the confines of the kitchen. In the process of writing this book, we have built relationships that are not quite possible to fit to the processes and protocols of academic life. We have been invited by our participants to quinceañeras, birthday parties, community advocacy events… These relationships with our participants (and now friends) have pushed us to grow, to question, to care, and to hold others more deeply. It is these relationships that are at the core of this book. We hope we have done them justice.

Serves 8

Pastafrola

INGREDIENTS

For the crust:

1/2 lb butter (room temp)

1/2 lb sugar

1 egg

1 egg yolk

1 tsp salt

1 tbsp vanilla extract

1 lb self-raising flour

For the filling:

1 lb quince paste

water, as needed

DIRECTIONS

1. Place the butter in cubes in a bowl. Beat the butter with the sugar until smooth. Add the egg, egg yolk, salt, and vanilla extract, and beat. Don't worry if it seems to curdle at first; it will smooth out.

2. With a spatula, gently incorporate the flour until well mixed and manageable with your hands. Just incorporate, do not knead like bread. Once combined, wrap in plastic wrap, and refrigerate for 30 minutes.

3. For the filling: cut the quince paste into cubes, place them in a bowl, add approximately 1 tbsp of water, and heat in the microwave at medium power for 1 minute to melt. Then, mash with a fork or a potato masher, being careful as the paste can heat up quickly and burn easily.

4. Remove the dough from the refrigerator, and press it into a tart mold with your fist. Arrange the edges, and fill with the melted quince paste.

5. For the decoration, roll out the dough between 2 pieces of plastic wrap and chill. Remove the top wrap, and cut strips with a knife, cutting through the bottom wrap. Lift the strips with the wrap, and place them over the filling. Remove the wrap.

6. Bake at 395°F for about 30 minutes, or until golden brown.

Catering

CONTACT INFO

TETIANA STRATILAT

(970) 305-6470 | @stratilat_tatiana

YRAIMA YLARRAZA

(720) 253-4429 (WhatsApp only)

SANDRA ARELLANO

(720) 447-2073

ANGELICA CRESPO

(720) 809-2316

ALEJANDRO FLORES

(303) 525-8840 | @alejandro.flores_munoz

CLAUDIA Y SILVIA QUIJADA

(720) 508-3197 | pupusaloverdenver@gmail.com

CARLOS BLANCO

(720) 999-1639 | @deliciousbaruc

JESUS & ALBERLI MARTE

(720) 471-5502

YOSBER ALEXIS

(720) 656-2110 | yosberalexisrios@gmail.com

Made in United States
Troutdale, OR
09/05/2024

22615703R00071